the
Kindness Handbook

Also by Sharon Salzberg

The Force of Kindness
Faith
Lovingkindness
A Heart as Wide as the World

the Kindness Handbook
a practical companion

⋙

SHARON SALZBERG

SOUNDS TRUE
Boulder, Colorado

Sounds True, Inc., Boulder CO 80306

© 2008 Sharon Salzberg

Published 2008

10 9 8 7 6 5 4 3 2 1

Library of Congress Cataloging-in-Publication Data

Salzberg, Sharon.
The kindness handbook : a practical companion / Sharon Salzberg.
p. cm.
Includes bibliographical references.
ISBN 978-1-59179-655-8 (hardcover)
1. Kindness. I. Title.
BJ1533.K5S256 2008
177'.7 — dc22
2008019329

Book design by Karen Polaski

Printed in Canada

✪ This book is printed on recycled paper containing
100% post-consumer waste and processed without chlorine.

꧁꧂

To the people of Tibet and Burma, who live with
wisdom and compassion for those who try to harm you;
the transcendent strength of lovingkindness;
and the integrity of nonviolence
that is made manifest every day

Contents

꧁

Introduction

It takes boldness, even audacity, to step out of our habitual patterns and experiment with a quality like kindness — to work with it and see just how it might shift and open up our lives. This book is an invitation to do just that. Kindness can manifest as compassion, as generosity, as paying attention. It can be offered to ourselves, to those whom we know and hold in high regard, to those whom we find difficult, to friends, to strangers, to all of life. For kindness to be more fully realized it needs to be distinguished from being ineffectual or meek. It needs to be infused with wisdom. Kindness needs to be supported by courage and threaded with balance.

Sometimes the practice of kindness brings ready, joyful results. Other times it takes an awful lot from us and is exceptionally hard — but it still feels like the right thing to do. Sometimes the most important recipient of kindness is the one most commonly overlooked — ourselves. Other times forming a dedication to care for others is the single most important thing we can do to experience and abide in our own genuine happiness.

This handbook is a collection of stories, meditation exercises, inspirations, poems, and teachings, all pointing to the power and grace of kindness. There are three main sections: The Foundation, which examines the fundamentals of lovingkindness, compassion, and a truer sense of happiness than many of us experience day to day; The Entry, which explores several different dimensions of love and compassion for ourselves, the oft-hidden ingredient that establishes kindness as a real possibility in our relationships, families, and work in the world; and The Expression, which carries kindness into multifaceted arenas in our lives, looking at how our deepest aspirations and day-to-day realities come together to remake our lives in the midst of ordinary circumstances.

Through its meditations, anecdotes, and readings, this book is designed to be used progressively if you wish, as a guidebook through the wide-ranging landscape of kindness. It can also simply be opened to any page — what is being presented on that page may help frame a contemplation on what is being presented in your life.

the Foundation

❦

*The Underpinnings
of Kindness*

As the Buddha said, "Just as the dawn is the forerunner and the first indication of the rising sun, so is right view the forerunner and the first indication of wholesome states."
Our view of who we are, what we are capable of, what matters in the world, molds our intentions, which in turn mold our actions. How we look at our lives becomes the basis for how we act and how we live and whether our choices are shaped by love and kindness. Transforming our understanding transforms our whole life: our happiness, our degree of connectedness, our freedom. None of these are fixed in the particular externals of who we are; they are held in the universal potential of what we might become.

The Search for Happiness

I have a friend who went to India a while ago, and the day before he was going to fly we had a phone conversation. It turned out he was going with another friend who had made all of the travel arrangements, and this person hadn't realized that for just a little bit more money they could have flown business class instead of economy class, which of course on such a long flight would have been far more comfortable. We were speaking about whether they could manage to change their tickets, if there would be a penalty, and how much nicer it would be to go business class. If they could arrange for the upgrade, they reasoned, they would arrive rested instead of exhausted and unhappy. Right in the middle of this conversation about moving into business class, my friend said, "I wonder how much it would cost to go first class?"

I know that state of mind so well. As soon as you get into business class, you start thinking about first class. This is how we are conditioned — there is always something else to want, even before we take a moment to appreciate what we already have, or are about to have. The variety of opportunity and circumstance is infinite. We get into a mind state of looking for an upgrade, and another upgrade, and yet another; it can be endless. Living more consciously is about turning around the habit of always wanting more. It is about deconditioning, about getting out of such constricted mind states and discovering a radically different kind of happiness — one that is not so vulnerable, that does not lead to certain dissatisfaction. We need to loosen our grasping and our clinging, and we need to have the courage to step out of our conditioning.

An essential question we might ask ourselves is, "What do I really need right now, in this moment, to be happy?" The world offers us many answers to that question: You need a new car and a new house and a new relationship and . . . But do we really? "What do I lack right now? Does anything need to change in order for me to be happy? What do I really need?" These are powerful questions.

When I have gone on retreat in Southeast Asian countries there is generally no charge for staying at the monasteries or the retreat centers, where all of the food is donated. Often it is donated by groups or families who come to the center to make the offerings. I'm sure that all of these groups of people offer absolutely the best that they can afford, but each day what is provided can differ quite a lot depending on the circumstances of those who are donating. Sometimes it is a lavish, bountiful feast. Sometimes it is quite meager, because that is all that the family can provide.

Time after time, I went into the dining room for a meal and looked at the faces of the people who had made the offering, since they commonly come to watch you receive it. They would look radiant, so happy that they'd had an opportunity to feed us, to offer something that would help sustain us. They seemed so happy that we were going to be meditating, exploring the truth, and purifying our minds and hearts on the strength of their offering. In that moment, when they were so genuinely grateful for the chance to give, I would ask myself, "What do I really need right now in order to be happy?" I realized that I was getting fed a lot more by their joy and delight than I was by the actual food.

The Dalai Lama has said, "If you are going to be selfish, be wisely selfish." In other words, if we carefully look at our lives we can see that we spend an awful lot of time looking for happiness in the wrong places and in the wrong ways. We yearn to be happy, and this is right. It is appropriate; all beings want to be happy. The problem is not in the urge, or yearning, but in our ignorance. So very often we don't know where happiness is to be found — that is, true and genuine happiness, abiding happiness — and so we flounder, and we suffer and cause suffering to others.

As I go through all kinds of feelings and experiences in my journey through life — delight, surprise, chagrin, dismay — I hold this question as a guiding light: "What do I really need right now to be happy?" What I come to over and over again is that only qualities as vast and deep as love, connection, and kindness will really make me happy in any sort of enduring way.

THE METTA SUTTA

This is what should be done
By one who is skilled in goodness,
And who knows the path of peace:
Let them be able and upright,
Straightforward and gentle in speech,
Humble and not conceited,
Contented and easily satisfied,
Unburdened with duties and frugal in
their ways.
Peaceful and calm and wise and skillful,
Not proud or demanding in nature.
Let them not do the slightest thing
That the wise would later reprove.
Wishing: In gladness and in safety,
May all beings be at ease.
Whatever living beings there may be;
Whether they are weak or strong,
omitting none,
The great or the mighty, medium, short or small,
The seen and the unseen,
Those living near and far away,

Those born and to-be-born —
May all beings be at ease!

Let none deceive another,
Or despise any being in any state.
Let none through anger or ill-will
Wish harm upon another.
Even as a mother protects with her life
Her child, her only child,
So with a boundless heart
Should one cherish all living beings;
Radiating kindness over the entire world:
Spreading upwards to the skies,
And downwards to the depths;
Outwards and unbounded,
Freed from hatred and ill-will.
Whether standing or walking, seated or
lying down
Free from drowsiness,
One should sustain this recollection.
This is said to be the sublime abiding.

THE BUDDHA
Translated from the Pali by the Amaravati Sangha

Love Is an Ability

When I went to see the movie *Dan in Real Life,* I gasped loudly in the theater as a I heard a good deal of my life's work summed up in one line: "Love is not a feeling, it's an ability."

In teaching lovingkindness meditation, this is something I continually try to emphasize. If we see love as a feeling, it is almost like a commodity — and likely we will judge our notion of that commodity all the time: "I don't have enough, it's not the right feeling, it's not intense enough, it is too intense . . ."

But if love is an ability, there is nothing to judge. As an ability, love isn't destroyed in the ravages of time and loss, insecurity or disappointment. As an ability, love is always there as a potential, ready to flourish and help our lives flourish. As we go up and down in life, as we acquire or lose, as we are showered with praise or unfairly blamed, always within there is the ability of love, recognized or not, given life or not.

This is the kind of wisdom born of going through life's experiences and paying attention instead of being half asleep. It is the kind of wisdom born from allowing life to teach us and move us and open us to truths, like this truth about the rather surprising and heartening nature of love.

Essential
Lovingkindness Practice

B<i>havana</i> is a word in Pali (the language of the original Buddhist texts) that is usually translated as "meditation." It more literally means cultivation, nurturing, creating the conditions to allow something to emerge, to come forth, to flourish. In this particular practice what we are cultivating is *metta*, which means lovingkindness or friendship. Metta meditation is part of the living tradition of meditation practices that cultivate spaciousness of mind and openness of heart.

Classically metta is taught along with meditations that develop compassion, sympathetic joy (the ability to rejoice in the happiness of others), and equanimity. Together these four qualities are known as the Brahma Viharas. Brahma means heavenly, or best. Vihara means dwelling or home. So the Brahma Viharas represent our heart's most heavenly dwelling, our best home. Metta is the foundation practice of the Brahma Viharas.

Lovingkindness is considered a concentration practice, which means that we have a chosen object of focus, and we continually shepherd our attention back to it once it has wandered. In metta practice the chosen object is a series of phrases, at first directed toward oneself. Whenever the attention wanders away from the chosen object, we gently return to it.

This process of shepherding our attention back to the phrases whenever it has wandered is the act of concentration. Imagine just for a moment the amount of energy you expend in contemplating the future, in obsessive planning, in ruminating about the past, in comparing yourself to others, in judging yourself, in worrying about what might happen next. . . . That is a huge amount of energy.

Now imagine all of that energy gathered in, returned to you, available to you. The return of that enormity of energy, normally dissipated and lost to us, is why concentration practice is so healing and empowering. We experience wholeness, the unification of our being, as we gather this energy back in. What is striking is the fact that this is our own energy; we don't have to contemplate the daunting task of somehow finding it or fabricating it. It is our own, but we ordinarily waste it.

When we practice metta, we relax, sit comfortably, and silently repeat certain phrases that emerge gently from our hearts. We hold each phrase in our attention and we connect to it. Traditional phrases are ones like (beginning with ourselves): May I live in safety, May I have mental happiness, May I have physical happiness, May I live with ease. Mental happiness refers to peace, joy. Physical happiness is health, freedom from pain. Living with ease implies the elements of daily life — work, family — going easily, without a sense of struggle. You can use these phrases or others that are more meaningful to you.

The phrases we choose are expressions of the very powerful force of intention in our minds. Every time we silently say one of the metta phrases we are harnessing the power of intention, which is the most important thing about this practice. The actual emotional tone we experience may change considerably: sometimes we feel exhilarated and grateful, sometimes uncomfortable and uncertain, sometimes we find the practice dry and mechanical. It is perfectly natural for your emotions to fluctuate as you do the practice. What is most important is to gently return to the phrases.

Developing lovingkindness toward ourselves is the first part of the metta practice. We repeat phrases that reflect what we wish most deeply for ourselves. People often find some difficulty in caring for themselves, in receiving love, in believing they deserve to be happy. We keep gently repeating the phrases directed toward ourselves because, whatever the emotional tone of the moment, as we practice we are purifying our conditioned relationship to ourselves.

We next send lovingkindness to a benefactor. A benefactor is someone who has helped us or been generous toward us or is inspiring for us. We visualize them or silently say their name to bring their presence forth, and we offer the phrases to them: May you live in safety, May you have mental happiness . . .

After some time we include a good friend in the field of our metta. Often we begin with a friend who is doing well right now. They may not be perfectly happy, of course, but at least in some arena of life they are enjoying success or good fortune. After some time of offering them lovingkindness we think of a friend who is not doing so well right now, who is experiencing some kind of pain or misfortune, and offer the phrases of lovingkindness to them.

The next category we hold in our hearts is a neutral person, someone for whom we don't feel a strong liking or disliking.

Sometimes we find that there are very few neutral people in our lives — as soon as we meet someone we tend to form a judgment of them. Sometimes we find that there are too many neutral people in our lives — outside of a certain favored circle of friends and family, people might as well be pieces of furniture for all the care we have for them. When we choose a neutral person and offer them metta we are offering it to them simply on the basis that they exist. They too must fundamentally want to be happy, and so we include them in our care as well.

Following this period, we begin working with metta for a person with whom we have conflict or difficulty. We usually begin with someone only mildly difficult, and then slowly work toward sending metta to someone who has hurt us more grievously. It is common to feel resentment and anger toward the difficult person; we do not need to judge ourselves for that. Rather, we recognize that our anger burns within our own hearts and causes us suffering, so out of the greatest respect and compassion for ourselves we practice letting go and offering metta. It is also important to realize that by offering metta to a difficult person we are not condoning their actions or trying to pretend it doesn't matter that they have hurt us or someone else. Instead we are looking deeply into our hearts and discovering a capacity for lovingkindness that is not dependent on circumstances and personalities. Of course this part of the practice is as challenging as it is liberating.

We finish the practice by connecting to the boundlessness of life and offering metta to all beings everywhere — all beings, all creatures, all those in existence. Whether someone is known to us or unknown to us, near or far, female or male, wise or ignorant, cruel or kind, they are part of this boundless fabric of life, and so we recognize our essential interconnectedness. This is the fulfillment of our capacity to connect to and care for all of life. We realize through our practice that a loving heart is our natural home, and through our practice we can always find our way home.

The Heart of Compassion

Compassion is known in Buddhist teaching as the quivering of the heart in response to pain or suffering. Finding the right relationship to pain, both ours and that of others, is very complex, because pain can be a tremendously powerful teacher and an opening. It can also be the cause of terrible anger and separation. We can be filled with loneliness and resentment because we're in pain; we can feel very isolated because we're in pain; we can feel a lot of guilt in a state of grief, blaming ourselves for something we did or something we didn't do or something we didn't say. We can blame ourselves for seemingly being ineffectual in a world that needs so much help.

Compassion allows us to use our own pain and the pain of others as a vehicle for connection. This is a delicate and profound path. We may be averse to seeing our own suffering because it tends to ignite a blaze of self-blame and regret. And we may be averse to seeing suffering in others because we find it unbearable or distasteful, or we find it threatening to our own happiness. All of these possible reactions to the suffering in the world make us want to turn away from life.

In contrast, compassion manifests in us as the offering of kindness rather than withdrawal. Because compassion is a state of mind that is itself open, abundant, and inclusive, it allows us to meet pain more directly. With direct seeing, we know that we are not alone in our suffering and that no one need feel alone when in pain. Seeing our oneness is the beginning of our compassion, and it allows us to reach beyond aversion and separation.

We can fool ourselves into thinking that we are feeling compassion when in fact what we are feeling is fear. Perhaps we are afraid that we could never do enough, and so we prefer to do nothing; perhaps we are afraid that our resolve will not see us through our efforts, and so we replace compassion with acquiescence. Perhaps we have slipped from compassion to hopelessness, and everything seems just way too much to deal with.

We might be afraid to take an action, we might be afraid to confront, we might be afraid to be forceful, we might be afraid to reach out. From the Buddhist perspective lack of effort is lack of courage. But this is not an easy thing to see about oneself, so we prefer to think we're being kind or compassionate rather than simply afraid.

We can fool ourselves into thinking we are feeling compassion and yet we might actually be feeling guilt. We might feel, if we see someone suffering while we ourselves are fairly happy or are happy in a way that this person is not, that we in some way don't deserve our happiness. But that is not quite the same as a sense of compassion.

Guilt, in Buddhist psychology, is defined as a kind of self-hatred. It is another form of anger. There are times when we understand that we have acted unskillfully, and we feel some concern and remorse. This can be important and healing. But a distinction needs to be made between such concern and guilt, which is a state of contraction, a state of endlessly going over things that we might have done or said. If we are motivated by guilt at what we feel, it will drain all of our energy; it does not give us the strength to reach out to help others. We ourselves take center stage when we are in the state of guilt.

Compassion is a practice of inclining the mind and of intention. Rather than laying a veneer of idealism on top of reality, we want to see quite nakedly all the different things that we feel and want and do for what they actually are. The mistake that most of us make at one time or another is to try to superimpose something else upon what we are feeling: "I mustn't feel fear, I must only feel compassion. Because, after all, that is my resolve — to feel compassion." So we might feel considerable fear or guilt, yet we are trying to deny it and assert, "I'm not fearful because I am practicing lovingkindness and that's all I am allowed to feel." The stability at the heart of compassion comes from wisdom or clear seeing. We don't have to struggle to be someone we are not, hating ourselves for our fears or our guilt.

One of the things that most nourishes true compassion is clarity — when we know what we are thinking and know what we are feeling. This clarity differentiates compassion from shallow martyrdom, when we are only thinking of others and we are never caring about ourselves. This clarity differentiates compassion from what might be thought of as a conventional kind of self-preoccupation, when we care only about ourselves and not about others. The Buddha said at one point that if we truly loved ourselves we would never harm another, because if we harm another it is in some way diminishing who we are; it is taking away from rather than adding to our lives.

It is tempting to undertake a meditation practice or path of development with the same kind of clinging motivation with which we might have undertaken anything else. Perhaps we feel empty inside, we feel bereft in some ways, we feel we are not good enough, and so we undertake spiritual practice to try to ameliorate all of that. But evolving a spiritual practice is not about having and getting; it is about being more and more compassionate toward ourselves and toward others. It is not about assuming a new self-image or manufactured persona; it is about being compassionate naturally, out of what we see, out of what we understand. Compassion is like a mirror into which we can always look. It is like a stream that steadily carries us. It is like a cleansing fire that continually transforms us.

Sympathetic Joy

Hearing about another person's success, we might think, "Oooh, I would be happier if you had just a little bit less going for you right now. You don't have to lose everything, of course; just a slight tarnishing of that glow would be nice." We react as though good fortune were a limited commodity, so the more someone else has, the less there will be for us. As we watch someone else partake of the stockpile of joy, our hearts may sink — we're not going to get our share. But the speciousness of that view is glaring: someone else's pleasure doesn't cause our unhappiness — we make ourselves unhappy because our negativity isolates us.

A friend told me about her envy of a woman who had it all. The "lucky" one had a good relationship, was a mountain biker and champion swimmer, and, because of her job, was often traveling to faraway places. My friend was single; she was challenged by something as simple as a long walk; she worked without prestige or glamour. And she felt scalded by jealousy whenever she thought of this other woman.

An alternative to feeling painfully cut off, all alone on our little island of resentment, is to develop what's known in Buddhist teaching as sympathetic joy, rejoicing in the happiness of others. Sympathetic joy is an unusual term — the word "sympathy" commonly means feeling bad for people when things go wrong for them. Learning to share the joy of others transforms our thinking about where we can find happiness. Usually we rejoice in what *we* get, not in what others have. But sympathetic joy is a practice of generosity, and giving isn't just about doing someone a favor — it also makes us feel better.

One doorway to sympathetic joy is compassion. Life is so fragile, with its volcanic shifts from pleasure to pain, from ease to difficult confrontations, from getting what we want to watching what we just got begin to fade away. We go up and down, all of us. Vulnerability in the face of constant change is what we share, whatever our present condition. If we remember that even people who have more than us suffer, we will feel closer to them.

My friend made an effort, and recalled the hardships in this other woman's life: Her brother was an alcoholic, her nephew was flirting with the edge of the law, and she was worried about money. Seeing the bigger picture not only enabled my friend to view the other woman in a new way, it also allowed her to appreciate the joy in her own life. As her perspective opened, she let go of old assumptions about how deprived she was. Now this woman no longer seemed so alien, and my friend could feel a burgeoning and genuine connection with her. The bindings of envy loosened, to her profound relief, and she felt joy for herself and joy that the other woman had good things in her life. Instead of seeing someone else's happiness as a threat to her own, it actually became her own.

Sit Like a Mountain — Equanimity

The fourth Brahma Vihara is equanimity, where the predominant tone is one of calm. In this spacious stillness of mind, we can fully connect to whatever is happening around us, fully connect to others, but without our habitual reactions of rushing toward what is pleasant and pulling away from what is unpleasant. Developing equanimity, in effect, is how we can forge a space between fear and compassion and between sorrow and compassion. This is how we cultivate lovingkindness without it turning into impatient entreaty or demand, "Get happy already, would you!" This is how we expand sympathetic joy.

Without equanimity, we might offer friendship only as long as our offering is acknowledged and appreciated, or as long as someone responds in kind. We would offer compassion to ourselves only when we weren't overcome by pain, and compassion to others only when we weren't overcome by their suffering. We would offer sympathetic joy only when we did not feel threatened or envious. When we cultivate equanimity, our tremendous capacity to connect can blossom, for we do not have to push away or cling to anything that may happen.

Sometimes in teaching meditation we say, "Sit like a mountain. Sit with a sense of strength and dignity. Be steadfast, be majestic, be natural and at ease in awareness. No matter how many winds are blowing, no matter how many clouds are swirling, no matter how many lions are prowling, be intimate with everything and sit like a mountain." This is an image of equanimity. We feel everything, without exception, and we relate to it through our own strength of awareness, not through habitual reactions. Practice sitting like a mountain sometime, allowing all images and feelings and sensations to come and go, as you reside in steadfastness, watching it all arise and pass away.

WE CAN DO IT

Abandon what is unskillful,

One can abandon the unskillful,

If it were not possible, I would not ask you to do so.

If this abandoning of the unskillful would bring harm
*   and suffering,*

I would not ask you to abandon it.

But as the abandoning of the unskillful brings benefit
*   and happiness,*

Therefore, I say, "abandon what is unskillful."

Cultivate the good,

You can cultivate the good.

If it were not possible, I would not ask you to do it.

If this cultivation of the good would bring harm
*   and suffering,*

I would not ask you to cultivate it.

But as the cultivation of the good brings benefit
*   and happiness,*

Therefore, I say, "Cultivate the good!"

THE BUDDHA
Anguttara-Nikaya

This passage is one of my favorites from the Buddha's teaching. I think it beautifully exemplifies the extraordinary compassion of the Buddha. The mind of the Buddha sees not good and bad people, but suffering and the end of suffering, and exhorts those heading toward suffering through greed or anger or fear to take care, to pay attention, to see how much more they are capable of, rather than condemning them. He sees those heading toward the end of suffering through wisdom and lovingkindness and rejoices for them.

It is a passage that inspires our sincere efforts. In the end, these ideas of how to live a better life aren't something to admire from afar or hold in an abstract way. We need to experiment with them, breathe life into them, see how they affect our minds and hearts, and see where they take us. Turning our lives in the direction of kindness can be done . . . It can only bring benefit and happiness. I can do it. You can do it. Otherwise, the Buddha would not have asked us to do so.

the
Entry

༄

Kindness Toward Ourselves

I was eighteen years old when, having recognized my confusion and unhappiness, I went to India to try to learn meditation. I was filled with self-judgment and the desperate wish to be someone other than who I was. After some time and travels, I went to Bodh Gaya, the site of the tree under which the Buddha had attained enlightenment 2,500 years before.

As I sat under the descendant of that very tree, what emerged from a deep place within myself was, "I want to have the love of a Buddha, I want to love myself and others the way the Buddha loved — without prerequisite or limit." I thought, "We all should know love for our vulnerabilities as well as our strengths, our problems and sorrows as well as our triumphs." That moment shifted all my ideas of what spiritual transformation would look like.

Instead of thinking that growth and understanding will come from doing battle with aspects of ourselves, or thinking they will come from enmity toward emotions, memories, and longings that we actually can't keep from arising, we discover that kindness and compassion for ourselves is the best and most healing trajectory for transformation.

The Shift to Compassion

Recently, as I was planning my travels from the East Coast to Hawaii in order to co-lead a retreat there with my old friends Ram Dass and Krishna Das, I considered many options. Krishna Das advised me, "Don't try to get there in one day, you'll be exhausted. Stop over somewhere on the West Coast, spend the night at an airport hotel, and go on to Hawaii the next day. It's the only sane way to do it." When I spoke to my travel agent, however, he recommended two connecting flights that involved only a two-hour layover in San Francisco, and that's what I ended up booking.

When the day of travel came, as I sat in the San Francisco airport and realized that flight delays would make it more like a six-and-a-half-hour layover — making my accrued travel time something like seventeen hours — I began to fall into a spiral of self-blame. I berated myself, "Why did you make such a poor choice? You're going to be exhausted. This was so stupid. You are so stupid." I quickly saw what was happening in my mind though, and letting go of those thoughts, I decided instead to enjoy the airport: the bookstore, the wireless connection, the food, the coffee.

When I met up with Krishna Das in Hawaii a few days later, I said, "I was so stupid. I should have done what you did." He replied, "No, actually, I was so stupid. By the time I got off my flight and into the airport hotel in San Francisco I couldn't sleep. After hours of trying I slept for about two hours, and then had to get up to catch my flight to Hawaii. I should have done what you did."

It was interesting to reflect that, looking backward, a perfectly reasonable choice can be construed as a big mistake, and any seeming mistake can provoke self-blame, or shame, or contempt, or kindness and compassion. Any trait we see in ourselves or others, any action, any emotional storm or frightened withdrawal, any failure, any experience of life's difficulties can be responded to in so many different ways. One response we can consciously cultivate is self-compassion.

Dr. Kristin Neff, associate professor in Human Development at the University of Texas at Austin, researches self-concept development, specifically the development of self-compassion. Dr. Neff describes self-compassion as having three main components: self-kindness versus self-judgment, a sense of common humanity versus isolation, and mindfulness versus over-identification.

She writes:

Self-kindness versus self-judgment. Self-compassion entails being warm and understanding toward ourselves when we suffer, fail, or feel inadequate, rather than ignoring our pain or flagellating ourselves with self-criticism. Self-compassionate people . . . tend to be gentle with themselves when confronted with painful experiences rather than getting angry when life falls short of set ideals.

Common humanity versus isolation. Frustration at not having things exactly as we want is often accompanied by an irrational but pervasive sense of isolation — as if "I" were the only person suffering or making mistakes. All humans suffer, however . . . Therefore, self-compassion involves recognizing that suffering and personal inadequacy is part of ... something that we all go through rather than being something that happens to "me" alone.

Mindfulness versus over-identification. Self-compassion also requires ... the willingness to observe our negative thoughts and emotions with openness and clarity, so that they are held in mindful awareness. Mindfulness is a non-judgmental, receptive mind state in which one observes thoughts and feelings as they are, without trying to suppress or deny them. We cannot ignore our pain and feel compassion for it at the same time.

It is useful to reflect on what inner environment is most conducive for us to be able to look at our distressing habit patterns motivated by love of learning, rather than fear of failure; what way of seeing ourselves and our difficulties provokes a willingness to risk new positive behavior, rather than staying mired in guilt over the old; what response enables us to avoid anger, loneliness, or bitterness when we recognize our pain or problems. What we discover is that the development of greater self-compassion, through the cultivation of mindful awareness and lovingkindness, is the way we can come up against life's inevitable frustrations, mistakes, and disappointments, love ourselves anyway, and keep moving toward growth and change.

Self-Compassion Scale

I found this research tool Dr. Neff developed both interesting and fun. You can, if you wish, do it periodically and get a sense of the self-kindness, sense of common humanity, and mindfulness you are bringing to bear in your life. If you feel dissatisfied with your score, try to consider this yet another opportunity to let go of self-condemnation and disdain and to practice self-compassion. (That is in part why I found it fun — you can't lose.)

RATE YOUR SELF-COMPASSION LEVEL

Please read each statement carefully before answering. To the left of each item, indicate how often you behave in the stated manner, using the following scale:

Almost never   Almost always

1   2   3   4   5

_____ 1. I'm disapproving and judgmental about my own flaws and inadequacies.

_____ 2. When I'm feeling down, I tend to obsess and fixate on everything that's wrong.

_____ 3. When things are going badly for me, I see the difficulties as part of life that everyone goes through.

_____ 4. When I think about my inadequacies, it tends to make me feel more separate and cut off from the rest of the world.

_____ 5. I try to be loving toward myself when I'm feeling emotional pain.

_____ 6. When I fail at something important to me, I become consumed by feelings of inadequacy.

_____ 7. When I'm down and out, I remind myself that there are lots of other people in the world feeling like I am.

_____ 8. When times are really difficult, I tend to be tough on myself.

_____ 9. When something upsets me, I try to keep my emotions in balance.

_____ 10. When I feel inadequate in some way, I try to remind myself that feelings of inadequacy are shared by most people.

_____ 11. I'm intolerant and impatient toward those aspects of my personality I don't like.

_____ 12. When I'm going through a very hard time, I give myself the caring and tenderness I need.

_____ 13. When I'm feeling down, I tend to feel like most other people are probably happier than I am.

_____ 14. When something painful happens, I try to take a balanced view of the situation.

_____ 15. I try to see my failings as part of the human condition.

_____ 16. When I see aspects of myself that I don't like, I get down on myself.

_____ 17. When I fail at something important to me, I try to keep things in perspective.

_____ 18. When I'm really struggling, I tend to feel like other people must be having an easier time of it.

_____ 19. I'm kind to myself when I'm experiencing suffering.

_____ 20. When something upsets me, I get carried away with my feelings.

_____ 21. I can be a bit cold-hearted toward myself when I'm experiencing suffering.

_____ 22. When I'm feeling down, I try to approach my feelings with curiosity and openness.

_____ 23. I'm tolerant of my own flaws and inadequacies.

_____ 24. When something painful happens, I tend to blow the incident out of proportion.

_____ 25. When I fail at something that's important to me, I tend to feel alone in my failure.

_____ 26. I try to be understanding and patient toward those aspects of my personality I don't like.

Scoring Sheet

SK: *Self-Kindness Items*

    #5   +   #12   +   #19   +   #23   +   #26   = Subtotal

_____ + _____ + _____ + _____ + _____ = _____

Divide subtotal by 5 for SK Mean _____

SJ: *Self-Judgment Items*

    #1   +   #8   +   #11   +   #16   +   #21   = Subtotal

_____ + _____ + _____ + _____ + _____ = _____

Divide subtotal by 5 for SJ Mean _____

CH: *Common Humanity Items*

#3 + #7 + #10 + #15 = Subtotal

_____ + _____ + _____ + _____ = _____

Divide subtotal by 4 for CH Mean _____

I: *Isolation Items*

#4 + #13 + #18 + #25 = Subtotal

_____ + _____ + _____ + _____ = _____

Divide subtotal by 4 for I Mean _____

M: *Mindfulness Items*

#9 + #14 + #17 + #22 = Subtotal

_____ + _____ + _____ + _____ = _____

Divide subtotal by 4 for M Mean _____

OI: *Over-Identification Items*

#2 + #6 + #20 + #24 = Subtotal

_____ + _____ + _____ + _____ = _____

Divide subtotal by 4 for OI Mean _____

Total Self-Compassion Score

1. Reverse code (rc) the negatively worded subscales (SJ, I, and OI) by subtracting each mean from 6:

   6 – SJ mean = _____ SJ(rc)

   6 – I mean = _____ I(rc)

   6 – OI mean = _____ OI(rc)

2. Add the six means:

$$SK + SL(rc) + CH + I(rc) + M + OI(rc) = \text{Total Mean}$$

$$\underline{\hspace{1cm}} + \underline{\hspace{1cm}} + \underline{\hspace{1cm}} + \underline{\hspace{1cm}} + \underline{\hspace{1cm}} + \underline{\hspace{1cm}} = \underline{\hspace{2cm}}$$

3. Calculate Grand Self-Compassion Mean

Total Mean divided by 6 = \underline{\hspace{2cm}}

Score Interpretations

Average scores tend to be around 3.0 on the 1–5 scale, so you can interpret your total self-compassion score accordingly. As a rough guide, a score of 1–2.5 indicates you are low in self-compassion, 2.5–3.5 indicates you are moderate, and 3.5–5.0 means you are high. Remember that higher means for the SJ, I, and OI subscales indicate *less* self-compassion before reverse coding and *more* after reverse coding.

Increasing Self-Compassion
Through Reflection

While it might seem that personal suffering is all too obvious, many times we actually don't pause to acknowledge our own pain, or if we do so we react reflexively by lashing out or quietly being filled with resentment. We know that we can extend compassion toward ourselves when the circumstances of life are painful and difficult to bear. Our tendency, though, might be to feel that we've failed or to feel angry, humiliated, or hopeless. We might confuse self-compassion with self-pity, and therefore try to avoid it.

Self-compassion exercises involve "stepping out" of our ordinary experience of painful feeling, taking a meta-perspective on our own experience so that we can consider it with greater kindness and a different perspective. Self-compassion is also relevant when suffering stems from our own actions, disappointments, or personal inadequacies. Many people say they are less kind and are harsher with themselves than they are with other people. Self-compassionate individuals, however, say they are equally kind to themselves and others.

Developing Greater Self-Compassion

To begin with, bring to mind a difficult life circumstance and observe the nature of different reactions to yourself as you picture that time in your life. How does anger feel in your body? How does humiliation feel? Do you notice other strands of emotion? How do they feel? Remind yourself that you are worthy of love, or you did the best you could, and notice how compassion feels.

Notice how various reactions affect your attention. Do you get obsessed, or does your perspective open? Do you have a sense of finality, or do you remember that all things change?

Ask yourself if you can be moved by your own distress, instead of falling into either being dismissive of it or being overwhelmed. Can you find the desire to heal and ameliorate the suffering you have experienced?

When recalling an aspect of your personality you dislike, notice how the perceived flaw is treated. Notice the emotional tone of the language you use to describe the problem. See what happens when, rather than attacking and berating yourself for being inadequate, you relax your tone, soften your body, and offer yourself warmth and unconditional acceptance. Notice what happens when you do this even if you have genuinely identified something as problematic and in need of change.

At the end of the session it is good to offer lovingkindness to yourself, then to those who have helped you and finally to all beings, all of whom want to be happy — all of whom are vulnerable and deserving of compassion, just as we ourselves are.

Shifting Perspective

As life presents annoyances, disagreeable experiences, and irritations, it can be a bold and creative challenge to meet these experiences with kindness and interest rather than a built-up stockpile of resentment.

This isn't meant to imply that we should be passive or complacent, or that we should sit around doing nothing to try to make things better. Rather, developing more kindness is a radical approach to help us deal more skillfully with conditions we may not be able to change, things that can weigh on us, distract us, or quite thoroughly ruin our day. This new sense of meeting the moment might actually open us to different, more creative ways of trying to communicate or working to have an impact on a situation that has previously appeared intractable.

At times we get fixated on what is unpleasant, and we lose the sense that there might be other ways of looking at the same situation. Yet we can step out of the box of our habitual reactions, have some fun with our minds, and greet what is happening with greater kindness.

When I am faced with displeasing or undesired situations and I need to create a sense of some spaciousness or lighten my mood, I try to remember this poem by Billy Collins:

ANOTHER REASON WHY
I DON'T KEEP A GUN IN THE HOUSE

The neighbors' dog will not stop barking.
He is barking the same high, rhythmic bark
that he barks every time they leave the house.
They must switch him on on their way out.

The neighbors' dog will not stop barking.
I close all the windows in the house
and put on a Beethoven symphony full blast
but I can still hear him muffled under the music,
barking, barking, barking,

and now I can see him sitting in the orchestra,
his head raised confidently as if Beethoven
had included a part for barking dog.

When the record finally ends he is still barking,
sitting there in the oboe section barking,
his eyes fixed on the conductor who is
entreating him with his baton

while the other musicians listen in respectful
silence to the famous barking dog solo,
that endless coda that first established
Beethoven as an innovative genius.

Contentment

The cultivation of contentment is also a way to cultivate kindness toward ourselves. I was once teaching at a center in New York City, in a lovely room on the tenth floor of a building. A friend who was attending the class sat close to the windows, which faced another building across a courtyard. She told me that as she was sitting there, feeling great contentment and ease of heart, and thinking, "There is nowhere else in the world I'd rather be, nothing else I'd rather be doing," she glanced across the courtyard and noticed a ballroom dancing class in one of the rooms in the nearby building. She immediately started thinking, "I should be doing ballroom dancing instead of meditating. That would make me happier."

When she told me the story I just laughed — it sounded so typical of our habitual seeking and restlessness, our easy dissatisfaction with where we are if we are not mindful.

It reminded me of my quest for the perfect cherry blossom viewing experience in Washington, DC. The famous trees, a gift from Japan in 1912, signal the coming of spring with their beautiful pale pink and white flowers. A few years ago, when I was teaching there, a friend took me to the Tidal Basin to see the cherry blossoms, but because of my schedule I could only go at night. It was glorious, but I kept thinking that something must be missing.

The following year I resolved to go during the day. Another friend was kind enough to bring me. I stood there, awed by the delicate beauty before me, until she said, "Oh no, they are past the peak." Suddenly I realized I was having an inferior experience (she knows she will never live down that remark). I felt a little let down, realizing that I had missed the "best" sighting, and I began to notice every little ragged edge and wilting petal. But it had looked perfectly fine before.

The year after that I was again in DC, and never once made it down to the Tidal Basin. I kept meaning to go, but somehow always found myself too busy. That was very disappointing. One day I was in a cab on my way to meet friends at a restaurant and passed some cherry trees on the street, in full and magnificent bloom. My heart just swelled at their beauty. Once at the restaurant, someone asked me if I had seen the cherry blossoms and I started to say no, meaning I hadn't made it to the Tidal Basin, hadn't seen an abundance of trees. Then I remembered the trees I had just passed in the cab and the joy the short glimpse had given me. Smiling, I said, "Yes. They were perfect."

Confidence

I first went to Burma to explore lovingkindness meditation in 1985. The intensive, systematic practice of lovingkindness was new to me, though I had been doing other kinds of meditation for years. The first day there, my teacher Sayadaw U Pandita called me into his room to give me some instructions, and he said to me right away, "Do you think you're going to succeed at doing this practice?"

My heart sank. I thought, "This is a trap. He's looking for conceit, he's looking for arrogance, he's looking for pride." I said to him quite meekly, "Oh, I don't know, maybe I will and maybe I won't."

He looked at me and shook his head somewhat dolefully. He said, "Everything you do, you should do knowing you can succeed in it. This is the basis for your practice, this is the launching power of confidence that we need in doing the practice."

What U Pandita was encouraging wasn't the state of arrogance or conceit or pride that I so dreaded him unearthing. He was talking about a state of heartful courage. The realization that we are all capable of so much is essential to our development in any endeavor, in our flourishing as full human beings. This calling forth of confident effort is the teaching of personal empowerment, of faith in ourselves. We can make changes in our lives, we can live consciously rather than mechanically, we can open our hearts and we can be more fully alive. It is taught that nobody can hand us happiness, but this also implies that nobody, on his or her own, can take it away from us either.

The tyranny of blunted aspiration, of thinking ourselves capable of so little, of resigning ourselves to habit and familiarity, isn't kind. We can so easily have a very limited sense of what we can do. Ordinarily it is only when we think of ourselves in extraordinary circumstances, like states of dire necessity such as a parent protecting the life of a child, do we imagine our inner strength. We rarely if ever imagine the depth and the richness of our own inner life.

The thought "I will never be able to accomplish this purpose; I will never be able to put forth that kind of unstinting effort" can itself be exhausting. The unacknowledged fear of failure can lead us to do a lot of complaining and is so demoralizing. To be kind to ourselves we need to open the scope of our aspirations.

This doesn't mean we need to have unrealistic goals, or punish ourselves through wild imaginings we in fact cannot fulfill. Rather, it is an encouragement to experience the joy of not holding back, of connecting to a bigger sense of possibility to experience the power of fully engaging, of participating unstintingly in our lives.

Delighting in Goodness

When the Buddha talked about cultivating the spirit of generosity, or the beauty of ethical concern, or a heart full of compassion, he also talked about reflecting on the good things we have done and taking delight in them. We recall acts of generosity, for example, not to bolster our ego, but rather to acknowledge that — in this world that offers so many choices and possibilities — we cared enough about ourselves and others to choose to give rather than to hold on. We recall and respect times when it would have been so easy to tell a lie, but we opted for the truth. We delight in times when we could have half listened to someone, but we gathered our attention and were fully present with them.

It is so easy for us to dwell on all of the regrettable things we have done or said — the times when we now feel we were too timid or too forceful or too withdrawn or too involved. I suggest you pause for a bit and think for the next few minutes about what you've done well, about a time when you were generous or kind or balanced, and try to appreciate yourself for that.

At first it might actually feel somewhat uncomfortable. It tends to be easier to think about the time we almost gave something but then decided not to, and it's still folded up in the attic. Or the time we were way too outspoken and said the wrong thing. Or the time when we carelessly overlooked someone, ignored them, and hurt their feelings. All these might be valid reflections, and helpful in some way, but they don't paint the picture of all that we are, all that we could ever be. Spending a few minutes each day thinking of the good within us and taking delight in the goodness we can manifest is how we are able to continually touch on and deepen a true and genuine happiness.

To rejoice in our ability to make choices, to cultivate the good, to let go of that which harms us and causes suffering for us, will give us the confidence to keep experimenting, to do things that might be somewhat new for us, that feel like taking a risk — not toward recklessness, but toward compassion.

No one of us can do these things perfectly; it is a constant journey, an ongoing practice. We practice generosity with others and with ourselves, over and over again, and the power of it begins to grow until it becomes almost like a waterfall, a flow. We practice kindness with others and ourselves, over and over again, and this is who we become, this is what feels most natural.

Lovingkindness Practice for Times of Emotional or Physical Pain

All our lives our innate wisdom tells us to let go, to be peaceful, to relinquish unwise efforts to control. Our culture, conditioning, and personal history usually tell us to hold on, to attempt to cling to people, pleasure, and accomplishments in order to be happy. Many times our lives are spent in a battle between our innate wisdom and the culture's message about clinging and control. When we are challenged by painful experience, it is above all the time to turn to, trust, and rest in the voice of truth within us.

Here are some phrases that may be of help to you in this. They are phrases of lovingkindness practice. Choose one or two phrases that are personally meaningful to you. You can alter them in any way or use ones that you have created for their unique personal significance.

To begin, take as comfortable a position as possible — sitting or lying down. Take a few deep soft breaths to let your body settle. Bring your attention to your breath, and begin to silently say your chosen phrases in rhythm with the breath. You can also experiment with just having your attention settle in the phrases, without using the anchor of the breath. Feel the meaning of what you are saying, yet without trying to force anything. Let the practice carry you along.

"May I accept my pain, without thinking it makes me bad or wrong."

"May I remember my consciousness is much vaster than this body."

"May all those who have helped me be safe, be happy, be peaceful."

"May all beings everywhere be safe, be happy, be peaceful."

"May my love for myself and others flow boundlessly."

"May the power of lovingkindness sustain me."

"May I open to the unknown, like a bird flying free."

"May I accept my anger, fear, and sadness, knowing that my vast heart is not limited by them."

"May I be free of danger, may I be peaceful."

"May I be peaceful and happy, at ease in body and mind."

"May I be free from anger, fear, and worry."

"May I live and die in ease."

the
Expression
❦

Kindness Toward Others

Spirituality is the movement from our prison of self-blame and self-preoccupation to an inclusive and open engagement with all of life. In many ways a spiritual path is essentially about connection — a deep connection to our own inherent capacity for wisdom and love no matter what, a connection to a bigger picture of life no matter what.

We can easily go from morning until night disconnected, not only from genuine contact with others, but also from more fundamental and loving aspects of our own hearts. Spiritual practices of meditation, generosity, service, and lovingkindness not only turn this tendency around toward genuine connection, they also become the manifestation of a free mind. Spiritual life is a place where the means and the end are the same.

Rules for Kindness

I was leading a meditation group in the DC area, and we had rented an elementary school auditorium for the day. All along the walls of the corridors were posted rules of being kind. During the breaks in the day, I would just stand and read them, again and again. They seemed so simple, yet like many simple truths, if we were to live them rather than merely admire them, they could change our life, whatever our age. The rules posted there rest on principles like dissolving the rigid boundaries we hold between ourselves and others, including rather than excluding, recognizing that our actions (and words) are consequential, and being thoughtful.

Carderock Elementary School rules for being kind:

- Treat people the way you would like to be treated.
- Play fair.
- Respect everyone—other students and all staff.
- Everyone can play.
- Help others when they need help.
- Don't hurt others on the inside or the outside.
- Honor all of the pillars of ethics.

I decided that every week I would take one of these rules to hold as a touchstone — a guideline — to remember, to make choices by, to experiment with deepening, to enjoy. One of the most provocative and poignant for me was "Everyone can play." When I first read it I imagined a child who was left out, who was staring at the in-crowd, feeling unwanted or unseen — then being beckoned forth, invited to join in, affirmed.

As I practiced this tenet, I noticed more hints of loneliness in those I encountered than I had seen before, more subtle echoes of that forlorn child than I expected. Including others was often like watching something unfurl and begin to flower within them. In making a point of including others in conversation, in regard, in a fullness of attention, I felt some subtle walls within me dissolve as well. There was a growing sense of rightness, of balance, because after all everyone should get to play.

Experiment with these rules; try one a week, or one a month, to emphasize. Even if you do live your life according to these tenets, consciously choosing to emphasize them can be enlivening, opening, and at times surprising.

Communication

There are these five aspects of speech by which others may address you . . . in a timely way or an untimely way. They may address you with what is true or what is false. They may address you in an affectionate way or a harsh way. They may address you in a beneficial way or an unbeneficial way. They may address you with a mind of goodwill or with inner hate. In any event, you should train yourselves: "Our minds will be unaffected and we will say no malevolent words. We will remain sympathetic to that person's welfare, with a mind of good will, and with no inner hate. We will keep pervading them with an awareness imbued with good will and, beginning with them, we will keep *pervading the entire world with an awareness imbued with good will — abundant, expansive, immeasurable, free from hostility, free from ill will." That's how you should train yourselves.*

THE BUDDHA

A friend once told me about repeated fights he had had with his wife early on in their marriage. Much of their conflict centered on how to have dinner. He liked to eat hurriedly, standing up in the kitchen, getting it over with as quickly as possible. She liked to set the table elegantly, sit down and eat leisurely, together. Many nights they fought instead of eating. Finally they sought the help of a marriage counselor.

As they examined the layers of meaning hidden in the simple and familiar word "dinner," they each discovered how many associations, and how many people, they were actually bringing to that table. He talked about his father, a brutal man who was often only home at dinnertime, which became a nightmarish experience to be escaped from as quickly as possible. She spoke of her fractured family and her mentally ill brother who consumed her mother with worry. It was mainly at dinner that her family made an effort to talk to *her*, to find out about her day — where she felt she indeed belonged to a family.

For each of them dinner was rarely just dinner, and their partner was often not the person standing in front of them, but an "other" made of an amalgam of past hurts and long-held dreams and tentative new yearnings.

Can we ever actually see another person? If we create an "other" out of our projections and associations and ready interpretations, we have made an object of a person; we have taken away their humanity. We have stripped from our consciousness their own sensitivity to pain, their likely wish to feel at home in their bodies and minds, their complexity and intricacy and mutability.

If we have lost any recognition of the truth of change in someone, and have fixed them in our minds as "good" or "bad" or "indifferent," we've lost touch with the living essence of that person. We are dwelling in a worldview of stylized prototypes and distant caricatures, reified images and often very great loneliness.

Meditation practice is like a skills training in stepping back, in getting a broader perspective and a deeper understanding of what's happening. Mindfulness, one of the tools at the core of meditation, helps us not be lost in habitual biases that distort how we interpret our feelings. Without mindfulness, our perception is easily shaped by barely conscious thoughts, such as, "I'm shaking and my stomach is roiling with what seems to be fear but I can never allow myself to admit that. I'll pretend it never came up." If we do that, it is a great struggle to be kind. There is no ready access to kindness without awareness.

Mindfulness also helps us see through our prejudices about another person. For example, a person might think, "All older women are fuzzy thinkers, so she can't possibly be as sharp as she is pretending to be." Mindfulness helps us to see by showing us that a conclusion such as that one is simply a thought in our own mind. Mindfulness enables us to cultivate a different quality of attention, one where we relate to what we see before us not just as an echo of the past or a foreshadowing of the future, but more as it is right now. Here too we find the power of kindness because we can connect to things as they are.

Making the effort to truly see someone doesn't mean we never respond, or react. We can and do attempt to restore a failing marriage, or protest at loud cell phones in public places, or try with everything in us to rectify injustice. But we can do it from a place that allows people to be as textured as they are, that admits our feelings to be as varied and flowing as they are, that is open to surprises — a place that listens, that lets the world come alive.

One essential step in learning to more genuinely see each other is to bother to look. If someone yells at us, or annoys us, or dazzles us with a gift, we do pay attention to them. Our challenge then is to see them as they are, not as we project or assume them to be. But if they don't make much of an impression on us, we have a different challenge: it is all too easy to practically look right through them.

In particular, the meditation exercise of offering lovingkindness (metta) to a neutral person confronts our tendency to look through people we do not know. We choose a person whom we don't strongly like or dislike; we feel, indeed, rather neutral or indifferent toward them. Very often it helps to select a near-stranger, or someone who plays a certain role or function in our lives — the checkout person in the grocery store, for example, or the UPS delivery person. We may not know much about them, not even their name.

When we send a neutral person lovingkindness, we are consciously changing a pattern of overlooking them, or talking around them, to one of paying attention to them. The experiment in attention we are making through these benevolent wishes asks of us whether we can practice loving "thy neighbor as thyself" when we don't know the facts about someone's dependent, elderly parent, or at-risk teenager, and so our heartstrings have not been tugged.

When we think of our neutral person, we haven't learned the story of their suspicious mole or empty evenings. We have no knowledge of their inspiring triumphs or their admirable philan-thropy, and so we are not in awe of them. We aren't seeing their tension after a disappointing job interview, or their sadness after their lover leaves. We practice wishing them well anyway, not knowing any of this, but simply because they exist, and because we do know the beauty, the sorrow, the poignancy, and the sheer, unalterable insecurity of existence that we all share.

On trains and on the streets and in our homes and in our com-munities we practice paying attention — through developing mindfulness, through developing lovingkindness, through letting go of projections — because a more complete attention proffers many special gifts. These gifts can penetrate through the exigen-cies of social roles, the seeming hollowness of chance encounters, and even through terrible hurt.

Paying attention in this way provides the gift of noticing, the gift of connecting. We find the gift of seeing a little bit of ourselves in others, of realizing that we're not so awfully alone. We can let go of the burden of so much of what we habitually carry with us and receive the gift of the present moment.

Through paying attention we learn that even when we don't especially know or like someone, we are nonetheless in relation-ship to them. We come to realize that this relatedness is in itself like a vibrant, changing, living entity. We discover the gift of caring, of tending to this force of life that exists between us, and we are immeasurably enriched by that.

Toddlers
Can Be Kind

I was reading the *New York Times* recently and came across this article, which made me think of the earliest inclination to help.

STUDY SHOWS BABIES TRY TO HELP

By Lauran Neergaard, Associated Press medical writer
Thursday, March 2, 2006 (AP)

Oops, the scientist dropped his clothespin. Not to worry—a wobbly toddler raced to help, eagerly handing it back. The simple experiment shows the capacity for altruism emerges as early as 18 months of age. Toddlers'

endearing desire to help out actually signals fairly sophis-
ticated brain development, and is a trait of interest to
anthropologists trying to tease out the evolutionary roots
of altruism and cooperation.

Psychology researcher Felix Warneken performed a
series of ordinary tasks in front of toddlers, such as hang-
ing towels with clothespins or stacking books. Sometimes
he "struggled" with the tasks; sometimes he deliberately
messed up.

Over and over, whether Warneken dropped clothespins or knocked over his books, each of 24 toddlers
offered help within seconds — but only if he appeared to
need it. Video shows how one overall-clad baby glanced
between Warneken's face and the dropped clothespin before quickly crawling over, grabbing the object, pushing up
to his feet and eagerly handing back the pin.

Warneken never asked for the help and didn't even
say "thank you," so as not to taint the research by training
youngsters to expect praise if they helped. After all, altruism
means helping with no expectation of anything in return.

And — this is key — the toddlers didn't bother to offer help when he deliberately pulled a book off the stack

or threw a pin to the floor, Warneken, of Germany's Max Planck Institute of Evolutionary Anthropology, reports Thursday in the journal *Science.*

To be altruistic, babies must have the cognitive ability to understand other people's goals plus possess what Warneken calls "pro-social motivation," a desire to be part of their community. "When those two things come together — they obviously do so at 18 months of age and maybe earlier — they are able to help," Warneken explained.

When I read this, I had a great sense of the poignancy of life: this inchoate, vulnerable, emerging sense of connection at such a young age; the many obstacles and tragedies that might come in the way of someone maintaining and developing their altruistic inclination. Perhaps we ardently work to make things better for someone, and they disappoint us with their refusal to change their own self-destructive behavior. Or we have been badly misunderstood and can't seem to alter someone else's view of us, no matter how we try. Or we have done everything we could to try to improve a situation, and what seems like the winds of fate bear down and shift everything in a way no one could have foreseen.

And then there is the triumph that appears when, no matter what our personal, social, or cultural conditioning, we again touch our ability to understand other people's goals. There is the sense of renewal that comes when we reawaken our desire to be part of a larger community, to relate to something bigger than our typically limited sense of who we are. There is the sheer life force — of engaging, of participating, of more fully connecting — and the exhilaration that comes when we are not bound by the strictures of standing apart.

Using inner practices such as meditation and daily-life practices such as generosity, we can cultivate this young, tender, shining altruistic potential throughout the course of our entire lives.

Kindness of
Being Yourself

In a classical Buddhist text from approximately 100 BCE, "The Questions of King Milinda," there is a dialogue in which the Indo-Greek king Milinda poses questions on life to the sage Nagasena. At one point King Milinda asks, "And how does faith leap forward?" Nagasena responds with an illustration of a large group of people, such as a village of people, who are on the shore of a flooding river. Their homes and their lands are all getting deluged and they are in danger.

Then one person comes along who has courage and strength and clarity, and that person sees a way to cross over to the other shore. And he forges ahead and does it. Just by seeing that one person can actually cross to safety, everybody else develops confidence in the possibility, and greater confidence that they too can cross.

In the example, the flooding river symbolizes our entanglements in habitual unhappiness, our tendency to be lost in the confused, conditioned mind. Crossing to the far shore, to the shore of safety, symbolizes our crossing to a place of awakening, of freedom. When we see that someone has crossed before us, or that many people have crossed before us, it can arouse a sense of inspiration: "Yes, they did it; I can do it too."

We turn for inspiration, inevitably, to models, to paradigms of humanity who convey wholeness to us, who convey another way to us, who convey peace to us. It is as though those who have realized a deeper truth bring to life a potential that exists within us that might otherwise have lain dormant because we simply did not believe in it. It is as though there is a fire within them that can light a fire within us. There is an urgency within them to be truthful, to wake up, to not waste their lives. That urgency within them seems to light a quality of urgency within us as well. And there's a peace within them and a confidence that also awakens those qualities within us.

These people have taken risks, they have made commitments, and somehow we join in their courage by being inspired by them. They uphold the energy of the possible for us, and they return us to ourselves, to our own aspirations to be living the best life we can.

There's a sense of timelessness in this. It sometimes feels to me like joining a stream. I think of all the women and all the men who for so many years, so many centuries, have walked a spiritual path, have gone forth, have let go of habit, have let go of the familiar, have faced down conventional ways of thinking, have taken a risk and seen a greater truth about life.

Each one of us is the next link in this chain, this transmission. When we are willing to make hard choices in morality, to not be swayed by the seeming ease of shading the truth and to resolve to live by our principles, work to care for all, continually look at our minds and hearts and go beyond the strictures of conditioning, we are crossing that flooded river. With our actions every day, and by being our truest self, we are a conduit of possibility for others. Just by living the best lives we can, the kindest, the most compassionate, we have done something to sustain and illuminate a path to freedom.

Motivation

We can never exactly know how our actions will ripple out and affect others. We may, through force of habit, disparage ourselves, considering an action to be inadequate, or resign ourselves to its seeming mediocrity, but we can't possibly know the ultimate result of anything we do. The poet T. S. Eliot wrote, "For us there is only the trying. The rest is not our business." This larger vision of life is what sustains our actions beyond immediate success and failure.

Usually when we assess the value of our actions, we do so in terms of whether or not they will produce a certain result — doing the good we envisioned, in the time frame we anticipated.

If it doesn't work out that way, we may lose confidence in what we do and grow dispirited. Unless we can guarantee the result we want, we might even decide not to take certain actions at all. Such attachment to achieving results can lead to relentless expectation, burnout, and the desolating habit of feeling we can never do enough.

We can be fixated on successful results, on the perfect achievement, on recognition in the eyes of others as the only hallmark of having done well. We ordinarily feel good about ourselves if our efforts are quickly praised, or if the results of our efforts are measurable and prompt by conventional standards.

However, being willing to take a risk, trying really hard in new terrain, learning to be wholehearted instead of diffident, courageously working to overcome setbacks instead of despairing, beginning again if we falter — these are often actions that we do not count when we are assessing our "successes."

In Buddhist teaching the immediate result of an action, and how others respond to it, is only a small part of its value. There is another significant aspect: the intention that gives rise to an action. The intention is our basic motivation, or the inner urge that sparks the action, and it is formed by our worldview — where we believe happiness comes from, what we think we are capable of, where we find a sense of meaning. The momentary urges that shape what we do are intentions, as are the convictions we hold and the aspirations for which we aim.

Intentions are not just about will, or about resolutions we make on New Year's Eve with some hope in our hearts; intention is about the overall everyday vision we hold of what matters to us, what we believe is possible for us. Intentions express the spirit of our activities, the emotional tone of our efforts. They come to life with each action we take.

An action can be motivated by love — or by hatred and revenge. Self-interest can be the source of what we do — or generosity can. Knowing the intention or motivation behind the action reveals what is really going on. A seemingly generous act born out of a tangled skein of self-hatred, or a feeling like "I don't deserve to have anything so I might as well give it away," is more a kind of martyrdom. A seemingly ethical act born out of fear has its center in rigid repression. Professing love for someone else through giving a gift when deep down we can't love ourselves easily becomes codependency, a distressing search for intimacy, a loss of boundaries — no matter how it appears on the surface.

If we are basing our view of the integrity of our actions solely on the results we see before us, and not considering the heart-space giving rise to and threading throughout what we do, then we have to ask, "On what basis, and when, do we measure success and failure?" Any ordinary favor we do for someone, or any compassionate reaching out, may seem to be going nowhere at first but may be planting a seed for later effects that we can't predict right now. Sometimes we need to just do the best we can and then trust in an unfolding we can't design or ordain.

If we develop the habit of noticing our intentions, we have a much better compass with which to navigate our lives. We can pay attention to what we are really hoping for, and what we are doing, and why we are doing it. As His Holiness the Dalai Lama said, "Motivation is very important, and thus my simple religion is love, respect for others, honesty: teachings that cover not only religion but also the fields of politics, economics, business, science, law, medicine — everywhere. With proper motivation these can help humanity."

Acting from Love

When facing someone's suffering and attempting to make things better, we can be moved by many different motivations: things like hope, clinging, generosity, fear. As human beings we often use outrage to escape from helplessness and despair. The sheer energy of anger can be very important in that way. It is as though our life force is asserting itself; we are drawing boundaries, declaring certain behavior unacceptable, and definitely (maybe at long last) refusing to be mistreated or allow someone else to be mistreated.

But if we get lost in the anger, saying in effect, "This is who I really am, this defines me," then we are vulnerable to tunnel vision, to perpetuating cycles of revenge and lashing out reflexively instead of acting consciously, or to being impatient and dissatisfied until we just give up.

We need to explore other motivating forces, to find one that is every bit as powerful as anger yet without its destructive force, one that will keep us going in our efforts. An example of this for me is Aung San Suu Kyi, leader of the pro-democracy movement in Burma, who was placed under house arrest in 1989 for her political activities. While still confined, she received the Nobel Peace Prize in 1991. Suu's sons were sixteen and twelve when she was arrested, and she was not able to see them again for years. It was over two years before she saw her husband again.

Describing her imprisonment, Suu writes, "I refused to accept anything from the military. Sometimes I didn't even have enough money to eat. I became so weak from malnourishment that my hair fell out, and I couldn't get out of bed." Despite the depth of her suffering, Suu later said, "When I compared notes with my colleagues in the democracy movement in Burma who have suffered long terms of imprisonment, we found that an enhanced appreciation of metta [lovingkindness] was a common experience. We had known and felt both the effects of metta and the unwholesomeness of natures lacking in metta."

This commitment to love as the motivation fueling our efforts for change and our response to injustice or the suffering of a loved one is the essence of enlightened social action and caring for others. Turning away from causing suffering, we turn toward the compassionate urge to bring about happiness and well-being for all. In the formal meditative practice of metta, we declare, "Just as I want to be free from pain and suffering, may all beings be free from pain and suffering. Just as I wish to be happy, may all beings be happy."

Imprisoned in her own house for years, Aung San Suu Kyi lived daily with the contrast between "the effects of metta" (the development of greater love for all) and the effects of "natures lacking in metta" (the dehumanization of herself and her colleagues). While lack of metta gave rise to suffering, the power of metta, both within her own mind and within the minds of others, gave rise to a wholly different place from which to work for change.

Qualities like love and compassion will lift our efforts beyond dualistic struggles between "us" and "them." Having a sense of a bigger picture of life will imbue our efforts with patience, encouraging us to keep trying beyond the initial, perhaps flawed, result we see in front of us. Realizing and then remembering that tomorrow doesn't have to look like today forms the basis of our aspirations, our hope, and our diligence.

We can affirm and then rely on those spiritual values, such as love, which lift our actions out of time, rigid duality, and expectation, without necessarily belonging to a religious tradition and accepting its tenets. No matter our belief system, we have the power to open our hearts, without dogma but with intelligence and discernment, to that which is bigger than our immediate circumstance.

We can nurture a new sense of our actions in many ways. In meditation, we can see, for example, how much everything and everyone is constantly changing, and we realize that in the midst of change we are not trapped, that there can always be a sense of possibility. This realization dissolves hopelessness. If, in times of suffering, we can still recognize the ties we have to others — that we all are vulnerable to pain and loss, whatever our present circumstances are, that we are still held by the flow of life itself even in our unhappiness, that in truth we are not cut off and alone — this power of connection awakens our love and the motivating force of kindness.

Just Leave It
with Them

Ihave heard that on one occasion the Buddha was staying near Rajagaha in the Bamboo Grove . . . Then the brahman Akkosaka ["Insulter"] Bharadvaja heard . . . Angered and displeased, he went to the Buddha, and on arrival insulted and cursed him with rude, harsh words.

When this was said, the Buddha One said to him: "What do you think, brahman: Do friends and colleagues, relatives and kinsmen come to you as guests?"

"Yes, Master Gotama, sometimes friends and colleagues, relatives and kinsmen come to me as guests."

"And what do you think: Do you serve them with staple and non-staple foods and delicacies?"

"Yes, sometimes I serve them with staple and non-staple foods and delicacies."

"And if they don't accept them, to whom do those foods belong?"

"If they don't accept them, Master Gotama, those foods are all mine."

"In the same way, brahman, that with which you have insulted me, who is not insulting; that with which you have taunted me, who is not taunting; that with which you have berated me, who is not berating: that I don't accept from you. It's all yours, brahman. It's all yours.

"Whoever returns insult to one who is insulting, returns taunts to one who is taunting, returns a berating to one who is berating, is said to be eating together, sharing company, with that person. But I am neither eating together nor sharing your company, brahman. It's all yours. It's all yours."

THE BUDDHA

In pre-kindergarten, the daughter of a friend of mine had a boy in her class who was very sensitive and had a tendency to be physically aggressive when upset. He and my friend's daughter became quite close, and he grew to trust her. One day at school he approached her to ask for her help. His opening comment was that he could see she was a good friend to people. He then asked if she could teach him how to be a good friend also. Her succinct response was, "Just try not to hit people."

This precise piece of advice reminded me of an article published in the *New York Times* on June 12, 2007, titled, "In the Classroom, A New Focus on Quieting the Mind." It described how during a five-week pilot program at Piedmont Avenue Elementary, the "mindful" coach, who visited every classroom twice a week, led fifteen-minute sessions on how to have "gentle breaths and still bodies." Students in a fifth-grade class tried to pay attention to their breath, and their coach asked them to "cultivate compassion" by reflecting on their emotions before lashing out at someone on the playground.

A student in the program, when asked to describe mindfulness, said that mindfulness is "not hitting someone in the mouth." His has become my favorite new definition of mindfulness, because I think it implies so much. It implies that we can recognize the anger or irritation we are feeling as it begins, not fifteen consequential actions later, only then to realize, "Oh, I was angry."

It implies having a relationship to our own difficult feelings and reactions so that we neither fall into them and get overcome by them, nor struggle hatefully against them. Those responses tend to escalate the difficult feeling we had to begin with, even if we don't want that. Defining mindfulness as "not hitting someone in the mouth" implies that from the space we are given from being mindful, we discover we can remember lessons learned before, and make clearer and better choices as to action. Maybe we won't accept someone's berating and insulting and taunting; we instead will just leave it with them, and remain free.

The mother of the young man who described mindfulness as "not hitting someone in the mouth" said at a session for parents, "He doesn't know what to do with his energy. But one day after school he told me, 'I'm taking a moment.'" If we remember to take a moment, in the larger context of not hitting people or lashing out verbally or acting thoughtlessly, we can shape our lives in the pattern of kindness.

We've Done It All

In a story told about the great Indian sage Neem Karoli Baba (Maharaji), a policeman was leading a captive through town and being very cruel to him. Maharaji said, "Don't do that."

The policeman spoke nastily to Maharaji, but Maharaji replied, "You should be more kind. You never know when you will be in the same position."

The next day the policeman was arrested for bribery and taken in chains through the town.

In terms of Buddhist cosmology, which has a worldview of beginningless time, we have all done everything. Those in any particular community, for example, throughout the course of many lifetimes are said to have been one another's children and parents, and enemies and lovers and friends. We have hurt one another and saved one another, lifted one another up and stabbed one another in the back. We've all done everything to and with and for and against one another. We've killed each other and helped each other and served each other, and we've all played every role. We've all done everything.

From that perspective, when we look at really difficult or cruel or terrible action, even as we recognize how wrong it is, we logically should do so without self-righteousness. We cannot righteously say, "I, who am so immaculate, way over here, are looking at you way down there, you who have done this terrible thing I could never ever do" — because we've done the same terrible thing at one time or another.

And so, even as we deal directly with wrong action and pain and hurt and try to stop it or redress wrongs, our actions can be done without hardening our hearts or feeling separate and superior.

Of course, this is not a system of thought or belief that makes sense to everyone. If it doesn't, there are many other ways to get a similar insight. I don't think it takes a huge amount of introspection to realize how many impulses and desires and fears and moments of aggression and hostility come up in our own minds. We certainly don't act on them all, at times because of our awareness, or training, or background, or understanding, or even sheer good luck (haven't you ever looked back on something you almost did and thought, "Thank goodness — that was awfully close. I barely escaped that stupidity"?). We may have the wisdom or the courage or the awareness or the opportunity or the grace not to follow these impulses. But to imagine that they don't even arise within us is simply unrealistic.

We can know right from wrong, we can take very strong action to protect ourselves or one another, to try to rectify injustice or stop someone from harming someone, and we can do all this from a place of connection rather than a place of division and condemnation.

Reflection on Lovingkindness
for a Difficult Person

> Whence is there anger
> for one free from anger,
>   tamed,
>   living in tune —
> one released through right knowing,
>   calmed
>   and such.
>
> You make things worse
> when you flare up
> at someone who's angry.

Whoever doesn't flare up
at someone who's angry
wins a battle
hard to win.

You live for the good of both
— your own, the other's —
when, knowing the other's provoked,
you mindfully grow calm.
When you work the cure of both
— your own, the other's —
those who think you a fool
know nothing of Dhamma [truth].
THE BUDDHA

As you do the practice of lovingkindness for a difficult person, it is useful to remember the principle of starting in the easiest way possible. Don't choose the most hateful, terrible, difficult person you can call up from your life, or the world stage, or from history. See if you can start with somebody who is mildly difficult, someone with whom there is some conflict, some dis-ease, perhaps someone of whom you are a little afraid.

This practice is meant to be done with a quality of interest, an ability to investigate, to look at our reactions without feeling crushed by them. Offering lovingkindness, even with an only mildly difficult person, can feel quite difficult. We aim to do the practice as an exploration, not with a heavy heart and a lot of self-judgment, but with an ability to look gently at oneself, at all the various resistances and places of holding back and not wanting to let go that we see.

Anger

It is useful to recognize that there can be a lot of clarity in anger. At times anger can cut through social niceties, and denial, and collusion, and pretense, to name some truths that might be hard to name and might not be very popular when spoken. But there also can be a tremendously deluding quality in anger. When we are lost in our own anger, we are lost in a very narrow definition of who we are, who this other person is, who any of us might become. We forget that there are possibilities inherent within the truth of change. We forget that everything is vastly conditioned, that no singular act is alone, isolated, apart from all the conditions that come together to make it so.

The metaphor from Buddhist psychology that's often used to describe anger is that of a forest fire, which can burn wild, leaving us devastated and maybe leaving us very far from where we actually want to be. The Buddha said, "Anger with its poison source and fevered climax is murderously sweet." It has both sides — the sweet relief of the energy, and the murderous side. Anger can give us a temporary feeling of strength, yet the devastation it wreaks can be immense.

Our effort must be not to suppress the feeling of anger, but to not have it be the automatic or inevitable place from which we act. Some of our effort is to feel the anger, feel the rage, feel all of it, and let it move through us without solidifying around it in terms of identifying with it, declaring it to be who we really are, who we will always be.

People often confuse letting go of anger with letting go of principle or a sense of right and wrong or a sense of one's value. It's really not so. We can use the energy and the clarity of that perspective without getting lost in the tightness and limitation and forgetting. That is the dawning of the strength of compassion rather than a kind of constricted, reflexive anger.

It is also useful to reflect that when we are lost in anger, we are the ones who are suffering. As I have heard the Dalai Lama say, "If you have an enemy, and you obsess about this enemy, then your whole life can become that obsession, that identification. And you're so limited. You can't eat well, you can't sleep well, you can't do anything else." And then he said, "Why give your enemy that satisfaction, of ruining your life?" Indeed, why not annoy your enemy by being happy?

Lovingkindness for those we find difficult is not about forsaking oneself, or acting as if everything is nice and everything that has ever happened is just fine — very likely, a lot of it is not fine at all. But, out of compassion for ourselves and out of real respect for what we are capable of in terms of a boundless heart, we practice. It is not that we want to pretend to like everybody or pretend to approve of everybody. Rather, it is all like an experiment. We see what happens when we recognize a connection with someone instead of feeling only alienation. We see what happens when we want to be freed of our own suffering. We see what happens when we pay attention to someone else's suffering rather than just their transgression.

After a time of practicing offering lovingkindness to somewhat difficult people we might be inspired to move on to include those whose actions have hurt us more powerfully. Often we have developed enough confidence both in the power of metta as the opposite of fear and in our own ability to generate metta to do that practice with some ease of heart. We have also explored and understood to a greater degree the difference between having compassion for someone and being passive or merely giving in. We've seen the need to balance love and compassion for someone else with love and compassion for ourselves.

If at any given moment, offering lovingkindess to someone very difficult for us is just too difficult or feels coercive, we drop it, and we go back to offering lovingkindness to ourselves or to a benefactor or friend. This isn't a cop-out or a move to substandard practice; rather it is exercising the openness and creativity the meditation practice actually calls for, and flourishes with.

Over time we may be moved to include a more difficult person again. In the challenge of doing so, we see so many things: caution, frustration, an effort to be in control, rage, fear, and also the chance to be different.

Even in horrible circumstances, we find that challenge and that prospect for meaningful change. I saw that after the Underground bombing in London in July 2005, when my initial response echoed most of those around me: sorrow for lives lost, distress at all those unheralded lives lost each day across the globe, some anxiety about getting on a subway in New York City.

Willa, my then seven-year-old goddaughter, had another perspective. Upon being told what had happened, Willa's eyes filled with tears and she said, "Mom, we should say a prayer." As she and her mother held hands, Willa asked to go first. Her mother was stunned to hear Willa begin with, "May the bad guys remember the love in their hearts."

Returning belligerence for belligerence, focusing on revenge, is familiar and easy but it tires us out. If we are willing to go to a new level of thinking, we discover that we are capable of so much more than we usually envision. No matter what our past, we can begin to be different; we can step out of cycles of reactivity, abuse or despair. Risking a new level of seeing enables us to try out new behaviors, like not shouting back or reflexively seeking revenge. Instead, we might use ways of communicating that convey our strength without damaging ourselves or those around us.

Imagine if we dropped our need to be right, our easy perpetuation of what we are used to, our need to be like other people, and actually tried to practice what the Buddha taught: "Hatred will never cease by hatred, it will only cease by love."

That would mean an enormous adventure of consciousness: a readiness to step into new terrain, redefine power, see patience as strength rather than as resignation. Perhaps it would mean protesting intrusions, and working to rectify injustice, and watching out for those we are responsible for, but in a way that allows life to be as textured as it is, a way that is open to changes. A way that listens, that lets the world come alive beyond categories of us and them, self and other.

This is a process of relaxing the heart and untangling it from fear and corrosive resentment. It is a process of recapturing our energy that may be held by a situation in the past and stagnating. It is a process of expanding our capacity to care, and to trust that caring will not deplete us or weaken us. It is a profound, challenging, and liberating process, and it is okay that it takes the time it takes. As someone once asked me, "Whose timeline are we working on?"

Generosity

The Buddha said that a true spiritual life is not possible without a generous heart. Generosity is the very first quality of an awakened mind. The spiritual path begins there because of the joy that arises from a generous heart. Pure unhindered delight flows freely when we practice generosity. We experience joy in forming the intention to give, in the actual act of giving, and in recollecting the fact that we've given.

If we practice joyful giving, we experience greater confidence. We grow in self-esteem, self-respect and well-being because we continually test our limits. Our habitual conditioning says, "I will give this much and no more, because giving even a little will deplete me," or, "I will give this article or object only if I am appreciated enough for this act of giving."

In the practice of generosity, we learn to see through our conditioning. We see that our conditioning is constructed, transparent; it doesn't have unchanging solidity. It doesn't need to hold us back. We can make clear choices about what is appropriate, not choices based on old fears.

Therefore, the practice of generosity is about creating space. We see our limits and we extend them continuously and consciously, joyfully, which creates an expansiveness and spaciousness of mind that's deeply composed.

Think about what it's like when the opposite is happening, when the mind feels brittle, narrow, confined, and dark. At that point, you feel on edge, uneasy, and you don't like yourself very much. By contrast, a vast and spacious mind doesn't feel so bound, contracted, and self-denigrating.

The aim of generosity is twofold, or else it's an incomplete experience. The first aim is to free our minds from the conditioned forces that bind and limit us. Craving, clinging, and attachment bring confinement and lack of self-esteem. If we're always looking for some person or thing to complete us, we miss the degree to which we are complete in every moment. It's a bit like leaning on a mirage only to find that it can't support us; there's not enough there.

When we are continually looking for the next experience and the next pleasure, it's like going from one mirage to another. We have no security. Nothing is holding us up. We practice generosity to free the mind from that delusion, to weaken the forces of craving and clinging so that we can find essential happiness.

We also practice generosity to free others, to extend welfare and happiness to all beings, to somehow — as much as each one of us can — lessen the suffering in this world. When our practice of generosity is genuine, when it's complete, we realize inner spaciousness and peace, and we also learn to extend boundless caring to all living beings.

For example, the Buddha said that when we offer someone food, we're not just giving that person something to eat; we're giving far more. We're giving them strength, health, beauty, and clarity of mind, even life itself, because none of those things is possible without food.

That single moment of offering someone food represents a tremendous proportion of the entire spiritual path. In an act of giving we're aligning ourselves with certain values.

Love is there in that moment because we feel good will toward the person who is receiving; we feel a sense of oneness with them, rather than alienation. We feel compassion in that moment, because we wish that person to be free from pain or suffering, to be happy.

In that act of giving, we rejoice in the happiness of someone else rather than feeling what we can so easily feel — envy, jealousy, and wanting them to be just a little bit less happy so we can feel a little bit more happy about our own state. In an act of giving, we want another person's happiness to increase.

In that moment of giving, we're abandoning ill will and aversion. Aversion creates separateness and withdrawal, a sense of not being at one with the other. Giving is an act of moving forward, of yielding, of coming forth, of coming closer. And we're abandoning delusion as well, because when we perform a wholesome or skillful action, we understand that what we do in our life — the choices we make, the values we hold — matters.

That's why the Buddha said that if we knew as he did the power of giving, we wouldn't let a single meal pass without sharing something. You can even do it mentally if you don't actually hand something over to the person sitting next to you. We can give in so many ways. We can give materially in terms of goods and money. We can give time and service. We can give care.

If we give a gift with this kind of motivation, without attachment to a certain result, without expectation of what will come back to us, it's like a celebration. It's celebrating freedom within ourselves as a giver, and also freedom within the receiver. In that moment, we're not relating to each other in terms of roles or differences. There's no hierarchy. In a moment of pure giving, we become one. We're not bound to the thought, "Well, this person has a lot more than I do materially, and so what difference does it make if I give them something?" We're not bound to the thought, "Maybe they don't like me. Here I am about to offer them something, and I feel really foolish," or, "I'd do this quickly except for waiting to be thanked." All of those habitual, confining thought patterns that might go on in a single interaction fall away in one moment of true giving.

Inner Abundance

SO MUCH HAPPINESS

It is difficult to know what to do with so much happiness.
With sadness there is something to rub against,
A wound to tend with lotion and cloth.
When the world falls in around you, you have pieces to pick up,
Something to hold in your hands, like ticket stubs or change.

But happiness floats.
It doesn't need you to hold it down.
It doesn't need anything.
Happiness lands on the roof of the next house, singing,

And disappears when it wants to.
You are happy either way.
Even the fact that you once lived in a peaceful tree house
And now live over a quarry of noise and dust
Cannot make you unhappy.
Everything has a life of its own,
It too could wake up filled with possibilities
Of coffee cake and ripe peaches,
And love even the floor which needs to be swept,
The soiled linens and scratched records . . .

Since there is no place large enough
To contain so much happiness,
You shrug, you raise your hands, and it flows out of you
Into everything you touch. You are not responsible.
You take no credit, as the night sky takes no credit
For the moon, but continues to hold it, and to share it,
And in that way, be known.

NAOMI SHIHAB NYE

My friend Krishna Das was once chatting to another friend, who at one point in the conversation admired Krishna Das's jacket.

Krishna Das promptly took it off and offered it to him. When the friend, incredulous and resistant, protested that Krishna Das shouldn't be without it, Krishna Das responded, "The world is full of jackets."

The best kind of generosity is said to come from a sense of inner abundance. With that vision of life, we recognize that in giving we don't lose anything, we are not deprived or bereft.

What's interesting is that there's no objective standard for this. There are poor people who have a strong sense of inner abundance. They feel that though they don't have much, they have enough to share and keep giving, even though from the outside it looks like they have so little. But they give what they can, with joy.

There are some wealthy people in this world who have a tremendous sense of inner poverty, and it's very difficult for them to let go of clinging to their possessions. Whatever they have objectively, materially, they feel internally as though they don't have enough. It's very painful; it's very hard for them to give.

There's a quotation from the *Tao Te Ching* that says, "One who knows that enough is enough will always have enough." Abundance is an inner sense. One of the great joys that comes from generosity is the understanding that no matter how much or how little we have by the world's standards, if we know we have enough, we can always give something. Then we can share, we can open, we can express lovingkindness. We can smile, we can offer someone respect and attention, we can care for them, we can be kind.

Our conditioning does not emphasize this. The dominant emphasis in our habituation is wanting, getting, and holding on. It doesn't emphasize the opposite qualities of yielding, letting go, and relinquishing. We are taught to believe we are not enough, we do not have enough, and we must accumulate and acquire experiences and people and objects to feel okay, or at least better. You don't have to go around and give away all of your clothing, but internally experiment with the audacious, delightful, and liberating possibility that the world is full of jackets.

Being Wrong

Ayoung friend once came to me seeking advice. He had been to India where he met a guru who had become very important to him. Now he wanted to bring his father from his comfortable home in America to that crowded, hot city halfway around the world to introduce him to the rather exotic guru. I thought about it for a moment, and then said to him, "You know, I don't think it's a very good idea. That particular city in India is very unpleasant. The food will be foreign, he may well get sick, and there will be annoying bugs. Besides, I myself found the scene around the guru kind of strange, and your father might well be repulsed by it. He may then dismiss all spiritual endeavor, which would be a terrible outcome. My suggestion is, don't do it."

The young man completely ignored my advice and did indeed go off to India with his father. When he returned a few months later, I immediately saw how very wrong I'd been in my counsel. His father just loved everything about India and felt right at home there. Not only did he admire the guru, he became a disciple of the guru. And not only that, he was determined to teach in the guru's lineage and was initiating a complete life change. My friend and his father were extremely happy. Having been proven so wrong in my advice, the question was, "Could I be happy for them?"

Sometimes kindness takes the form of stepping aside, letting go of our need to be right, and just being happy for someone. Their choices may not be hurting anyone, but may be different from the choices we would (rightly or wrongly) wish upon them.

As in the story above, sometimes we feel a need to be proven right as we look at someone else's life choices; it is not that they are necessarily doing anything wrong or hurtful, but they may be living differently from how we have decided they should be living. Or perhaps our advice turns out to be unappreciated or incorrect, as mine was, and we come face to face with the fact that someone's happiness does not revolve around us and our fabulous prescience and good sense — instead, it is based on their own, or even on sheer good luck. Can we let go of our need to try to dominate people's lives and our determination of what the correct outcome of their decisions should be? Can we simply be happy for them?

Sitting with my young friend and hearing about the glorious experience of his father's trip to India, I saw the cascade of emotions in my mind — embarrassment, skepticism, a touch of derision, and even a little resentment — and I knew I had a choice. Letting those feelings go without seizing them and building on them in a fit of misplaced righteousness opened me to real and powerful delight. Sometimes I intentionally ask myself the question, "What would I gain from this person's loss?" and it is quite clear to me that I don't benefit at all from someone else's pain. The true benefit is in stepping away from center stage and the kindness of delighting in someone else's good experience.

Community

Jean Vanier, founder of L'Arche Communities, says L'Arche is a place where "people, whatever their race, culture, abilities, or disabilities, can find a place and reveal their gifts to the world. You know as I do that we all begin in weakness and end in weakness. We are all broken in some way. The only answer to life is to love each other."

Vanier says that community life with the disabled has taught him what it means to be human: "The whole pain of our world today is the pain of walls."

I thought of the many layers of meaning in the word "community" when I read the following in the newspaper:

ILLEGAL IMMIGRANT RESCUES BOY IN DESERT

By Terry Tang, Associated Press writer

Saturday, November 24, 2007 1:27 AM ET (AP)

A 9-year-old boy looking for help after his mother crashed their van in the southern Arizona desert was rescued by a man entering the U.S. illegally, who stayed with him until help arrived the next day, an official said.

The 45-year-old woman, who eventually died while awaiting help, had been driving on a U.S. Forest Service road in a remote area just north of the Mexican border when she lost control of her van on a curve on Thanksgiving, Santa Cruz County Sheriff Tony Estrada said.

The van vaulted into a canyon and landed 300 feet from the road, he said. The woman, from Rimrock, north of Phoenix, survived the impact but was pinned inside, Estrada said.

Her son, unhurt but disoriented, crawled out to get help and was found about two hours later by Jesus Manuel Cordova, 26, of Magdalena de Kino in the northern Mexican state of Sonora. Unable to pull the mother out, he comforted the boy while they waited for help.

The woman died a short time later.

"He stayed with him, told him that everything was going to be all right," Estrada said. As temperatures dropped, he gave him a jacket, built a bonfire and stayed with him until about 8 a.m. Friday, when hunters passed by and called authorities, Estrada said. The boy was flown to University Medical Center in Tucson as a precaution but appeared unhurt.

"We suspect that they communicated somehow, but we don't know if he knows Spanish or if the gentleman knew English," Estrada said of the boy.

"For a 9-year-old it has to be completely traumatic, being out there alone with his mother dead," Estrada said. "Fortunately for the kid, [Cordova] was there. That was his angel."

Cordova was taken into custody by Border Patrol agents, who were the first to respond to the call for help. He had been trying to walk into the U.S. when he came across the boy.

The boy and his mother were in the area camping, Estrada said. The woman's husband, the boy's father, had died only two months ago. The names of the woman and her son were not being released until relatives were notified.

Cordova likely saved the boy, Estrada said, and his actions should remind people not to quickly characterize illegal immigrants as criminals.

"They do get demonized for a lot of reasons, and they do a lot of good. Obviously this is one example of what an individual can do," he said.

I was filled with sadness as I read it: for the boy, for his mother and father who had died, for Mr. Cordova. And quite grateful that Mr. Cordova could give up whatever dreams or ambitions he might have had to stay with a bereft, traumatized child. Sometimes kindness comes at great cost to oneself.

Rigidly categorizing those we encounter as good or bad or perfect or beneath contempt helps us feel secure. But if we look around, we realize that relating in that way doesn't allow us to really connect to anyone, and we actually feel terribly alone.

As human beings we have an incredible capacity for growth, understanding, and love. Though we might often get venal and angry and closed down, we can also give of the heart and show mercy. We can take time out before reacting and make an effort to see ourselves and one another more clearly. Even if we don't like someone or don't really know them, we can recognize their humanity and thus their complexity and mutability.

We can explore other ways of seeing: confronting the stereotypes we often hold of anyone who appears to be unlike us, the indifference we assume toward those we don't know. We can examine all the ways we create an "other" unworthy of our care, with people or nature or religions or nations. Doing this will continually undermine the walls our conditioning has constructed and open us beyond their pain.

A Vision of
Interconnectedness

I t really boils down to this: that all life is interrelated. We are all caught in an inescapable network of mutuality, tied into a single garment of destiny. Whatever affects one directly, affects all indirectly. We are made to live together because of the interrelated structure of reality. Did you ever stop to think that you can't leave for your job in the morning without being dependent on most of the world? You get up in the morning and go to the bathroom and reach over for the sponge, and that's handed to you by a Pacific islander. You reach for a bar of soap, and that's given to you at the hands of a Frenchman. And then you go into the kitchen to drink your coffee for the morning, and *that's poured into your cup by a South American. And maybe you want tea: that's poured into your cup by a Chinese. Or maybe you're desirous of having cocoa for breakfast, and that's poured into your cup by a West African. And then you reach over for your toast, and that's given to you at the hands of an English-speaking farmer, not to mention the baker. And before you finish eating breakfast in the morning, you've depended on more than half of the world. This is the way our universe is structured, this is its interrelated quality. We aren't going to have peace on earth until we recognize this basic fact of the interrelated structure of all reality.*

MARTIN LUTHER KING JR.

If our actions are infused with a vision of interconnectedness, then love and kindness will keep us going in our efforts. Interconnectedness isn't an abstract, fanciful notion, but a direct seeing of a deeper reality.

Consider for a moment something like a tree. We think of that tree as a distinctly defined object, standing there just by itself. But on another level of perception, the tree is not so completely separate. It is also the consequence — the manifestation or the function — of an extremely subtle net of relationships.

The tree is affected by the rain that falls upon it, by the wind that moves through and around it. It is affected by the soil that nourishes it and sustains it. It is affected by the weather and by the sunlight and by the moonlight and by the quality of the air.

Environmental awareness shows us that there is no "us" and "them." What happens "over there" does indeed have an effect on what happens to us "over here." Economics shows us this; epidemiology shows us this.

The first time I heard of AIDS, it was described to me as an exotic and rare disease affecting Haitian immigrants. At that time I didn't know anyone from Haiti, and so I didn't imagine that I would know anybody who might die from that particular disease. The first time I heard of SARS (severe, acute respiratory syndrome), I didn't make that assumption at all. It isn't only the planetary crash course in epidemiology we all have undergone that changed my outlook; it's the growing realization that what happens "there" or to "them" can and will affect "us" as well. We're not nearly as separate as we might think we are.

This is both good news and bad news. The bad news is exemplified in the environmental devastation of our time. Mismanagement, recklessness, or cruel disregard in one region can affect air quality, flooding, migratory patterns, and biodiversity across continents. It is exemplified in the global spread of disease by international travelers, drawn by need, commerce, service, or a sense of adventure. What happens in one place is consequential elsewhere precisely because we are interconnected.

The good news is that the same law of interconnectedness asks us to let go of rigid differences, to be responsive to the needs of others, to know that taking care of others is an inextricable part of truly taking care of ourselves.

The fact that everyone and everything has an effect on their surroundings is a call to honor our interconnection and show compassion toward all other beings. Respecting this interconnection can open us to an unstudied altruism that is simply a reflection of a more honest life. When we know how intertwined our lives are, we know that the lives of an ill person in China, a woman hungering for education in Afghanistan, a child in South Africa who walks for a day and a half at Christmas to receive the bag of chips and can of soda Nelson Mandela gives away, all have something to do with our own lives.

We can't avert our eyes, looking around those who suffer, those who are hungry, those who are ill or frightened. We can't look through them, seeking a more pleasing vista. We can't go along oblivious, shoving aside images of yearning, of terror, of resignation in a child's eyes somewhere far away, determined to forget that we glimpsed those things at all. Our picture of life necessarily includes concern for everybody, because that's the simple truth of how we can achieve safety and peace.

There are times when we can be cut off from reality. But we need to take the time to have an understanding of the layers of conditions coming together for even one meal: the people growing our food, the animals giving up their milk, the planet nurturing us all.

We can have a different sense of the interdependence in which we live, and the fallacy of an unbending sense of separation, of self and other. So many conditions and influences and connections and relationships help to make the meal what it is. It is the same for a homeless person, or for a survivor of domestic violence, or for an adversary, or for us.

In Mahayana Buddhism there is a famous teaching image that conveys this sense. It is called Indra's Net, and in the image the universe is depicted as an enormous net. In one place, where you can imagine the strings of the net meeting right at the nexus, there's a jewel — a highly polished, multifaceted jewel, like a diamond or a piece of crystal. Now, imagine in this infinite net at every place where there is that joining, there's another jewel just like that original one. In each of these places there's a jewel that is reflecting every other jewel all at the same time. If you look at one thing, you see all things.

In day-to-day life this translates into a much more realistic perception of the larger patterns and confluences of which we are all a part. This clarity of perception is the root of understanding. It's also the root of compassion and the root of engaged action born of love and kindness.

Forever

We humans are social beings. We come into the world as the result of others' actions. We survive here in dependence on others. Whether we like it or not, there is hardly a moment of our lives when we do not benefit from others' activities. For this reason, it is hardly surprising that most of our happiness arises in the context of our relationship with others. Nor is it so remarkable that our greatest joy should come when we are motivated by concern for others. But that is not all. We find that not only do altruistic actions bring about happiness, but they also lessen our experience of suffering.

Here I am not suggesting that the individual whose actions are motivated by the wish to bring others happiness necessarily meets with less misfortune than the one who does not. Sickness, old age, and mishaps of one sort or another are the same for us all. But the sufferings which undermine our internal peace — anxiety, frustration, disappointment — are definitely less. In our concern for others, we worry less about ourselves. When we worry less about ourselves, the experience of our own suffering is less intense.

THE DALAI LAMA

A few years ago I went to Tucson to hear the Dalai Lama teach. I arranged everything to go a day early in order to be able to give a talk in Tucson before the teachings by the Dalai Lama began. My plans were challenged, however, when I found myself in an airplane sitting on a runway for four hours at LaGuardia airport. Looking back on it, I sometimes refer jokingly to those hours as "the breakdown of civilization." It was hot, and it grew hotter. After a point, people started yelling, "Let me off this plane." The pilot resorted to getting on the PA system and saying sternly, "No one is getting off this plane."

I wasn't feeling all that chipper myself. I couldn't seem to get in touch with the people in Tucson who were supposed to pick me up at the airport, and I was concerned about them. I had an apartment to go to in New York City, and kept thinking, to no avail, "I can just go back there, and try again tomorrow." I was hot. I felt pummeled by the people shouting around me.

Then I recalled an image that Bob Thurman, professor of Buddhist studies at Columbia University, often uses to describe the flow of kindness and compassion that comes from seeing the world more truthfully. He says, "Imagine you are on the New York City subway, and these Martians come and zap the subway car so that those of you in the car are going to be together . . . forever." What do we do? If someone is hungry we feed them. If someone is freaking out, we try to calm them down. We might not at all like everybody, or approve of them — but we are going to be together forever, and we need to respond with the wisdom of how interrelated our lives are, and will remain.

Sitting on that airplane, I was struck by the recollection of Bob's story. I looked around the cabin, and thought, "Maybe these are my people."

It was fascinating to note that my impatience —"Couldn't you be a little quieter?"— and distress —"How much longer is this going to last?"— changed to taking a greater interest in those with me: Who are these people? Is it really imperative that they be on time? What is awaiting them? I watched the interplay of forces in my own mind as interest opened the door to a measure of kindness, and as "How much longer?" encountered "Forever," I saw my worldview shift from "me" and "them" to "we."

Lovingkindness
for Caregivers

R esearchers are finding that there is a growing interest in the relationship between positive emotions like compassion, kindness, gratitude, and altruism and happiness, health, and longevity. In the Works of Love e-newsletter of January 1, 2008, Dr. Stephen Post wrote: "The evidence . . . supports the following hypothesis: One of the healthiest things a person can do is to step back from self-preoccupation and self-worry, as well as from hostile and bitter emotions, and there is no more obvious way of doing this than focusing attention on helping others."

But it is also true that in focusing attention on others we may feel overwhelmed by the suffering we encounter; we may lose our own sense of meaning because we are so stressed. We may forget to take care of ourselves, and what was once a vital, generative form of giving or service might become an activity that depletes us or fills us with unbearable distress. When I did a workshop for nurses at Walter Reed Hospital in Washington, DC, one of the nurses told me, "The nurses who do well here are the ones who can focus on the resiliency of the human spirit. If you are overwhelmed by the sorrow of it all, you end up leaving quickly."

This tendency to offer care to others to an overwhelming degree is seen in many stories of family members of Alzheimer's patients who are unable to find enough support. It is seen in occupations where one repeatedly encounters trauma — firefighters, domestic-violence shelter workers, sexual violence counselors — and many other kinds of work where one daily sees an enormous, sometimes unfathomable degree of suffering. And it is seen when our caregiving is motivated less by altruism and more by old habits, some kind of coercion, or frank or subtle abuse.

Balance seems to be the key to a life of kindness, a life that sustains our own flourishing alongside whatever contribution we can make to the well-being of others. We need to have a healthy sense of boundaries. We need to remember self-care and the power of joy. Perhaps we need to change focus and make a point of appreciating the smile of a child, even as we are working to ameliorate a terrible and seemingly intractable problem. We need to connect and reconnect to whatever gives us a sense of meaning. We need to know what we cannot control and be filled with compassion anyway. Then we will have joined wisdom to kindness.

Lovingkindness Meditation
for Caregivers

Whether you care for a young child, an aging parent, a rambunctious teenager, a client at work whose needs are pressing upon you, or a community that proffers many responsibilities, any skillful relationship of caregiving relies on balance — the balance between opening one's heart endlessly and accepting the limits of what one can do. The balance between compassion and equanimity. Compassion is the trembling or the quivering of the heart in response to suffering. Equanimity is a spacious stillness that can accept things as they are. The balance of compassion and equanimity allows us to care, and yet not get overwhelmed and unable to cope because of that caring.

This is a lovingkindness meditation particularly for caregivers. The phrases we use reflect this balance between compassion and equanimity. Choose one or two phrases that are personally meaningful to you. Some options are offered below. You can alter them in any way or use others that you have created because of their unique personal significance.

To begin the practice, take as comfortable a position as possible, sitting or lying down. Take a few deep soft breaths to let your body settle. Bring your attention to your breath and begin to silently say your chosen phrases over and over again, in rhythm with the breath. You can also experiment with just having your attention settle in the phrases, without using the anchor of the breath. Feel the meaning of what you are saying, yet without trying to force anything. Let the practice carry you along.

"May I offer my care and presence without conditions, knowing they may be met by gratitude, anger, or indifference."

"May I find the inner resources to truly be able to give."

"May I remain in peace and let go of expectations."

"May I offer love, knowing I can't control the course of life, suffering, or death."

"I care about your pain, yet cannot control it."

"I wish you happiness and peace, but cannot make your choices for you."

"May I see my limits compassionately, just as I view the limitations of others."

Life Lessons

I think I mentioned before that some time ago my brother and I were driving one evening to Chattanooga, Tennessee, from Atlanta. He was driving the car. And for some reason the drivers were very discourteous that night. They didn't dim their lights; hardly any driver that passed by dimmed his lights. And I remember very vividly, my brother A. D. looked over and in a tone of anger said: "I know what I'm going to do. The next car that comes along here and refuses to dim the lights, I'm going to fail to dim mine and pour them on in all of their power." And I looked at him right quick and said: "Oh no, don't do that. There'd be too much light on this highway, and it will end up in mutual destruction for all. Somebody got to have some sense on this highway."

Somebody must have sense enough to dim the lights, and that is the trouble, isn't it? That as all of the civilizations of the world move up the highway of history, so many civilizations, having looked at other civilizations that refused to dim the lights, and they decided to refuse to dim theirs. And Toynbee tells that out of the twenty-two civilizations that have risen up, all but about seven have found themselves in the junkheap of destruction. It is because civilizations fail to have sense enough to dim the lights... And we will all end up destroyed because nobody had any sense on the highway of history.

Somewhere somebody must have some sense... must see that force begets force, hate begets hate, toughness begets toughness. And it is all a descending spiral, ultimately ending in destruction for all and everybody. Somebody must have sense enough and morality enough to cut off the chain of hate and the chain of evil in the universe. And you do that by love.

MARTIN LUTHER KING JR.

We can each be the one to dim the lights, to dare to be different. We can imagine a world based on love instead of hate; we can beckon a day where our own happiness and the happiness of others are seen as one, through the power of kindness. Holding this immense vision, we center our attention in the step-by-step work of making it real.

Reflections

~ **We don't need to be defined by our daily circumstances.** We often limit our sense of who we are to our roles, our jobs, our likes and dislikes, our rivalries, and our fears. When we learn to trust a deeper experience of who we are, we find our lives are far bigger, far more filled with potential than we usually imagine. We can find a sense of meaning in qualities like kindness, which are not bound to particular circumstances.

~ **We can learn to differentiate between inner voices.** There are those voices that are habitual, constricting, belittling — voices that hold us down. Then there are those voices that lead us on to happiness, peace, connection, voices that work for our healing and our good. When we listen quietly we can sense the difference.

~ **We can trust the reality of change.** If we look closely enough at any painful emotion or difficult situation, we see that it is bound to change; it is not as solid and inert as it might have seemed. The anger we feel in the morning may be gone a little later. Hopelessness may be replaced by calm. Even while a difficult situation is happening, it is shifting, varied, alive. Once we see the inherent change in our experience, we see that we are not trapped, that we can have options. We can sense possibility, however faint.

~ **We all have faith in something.** For some of us it might be sense pleasure, intoxication, or constant work that seems the way to attain happiness. For others, loving our neighbor is what gives us a sense of meaning. Often the objects of our faith are unconscious or have been handed to us by a tradition. When we make them conscious, we can examine whether or not they do in fact bring us happiness. Then we can choose to place our faith in those things that sustain us through the ups and downs of life, those qualities of the heart that are enduring, such as the power of kindness.

- **We don't really know for sure what will happen next.** When we leave the house for work in the morning, we make assumptions about what our experience will be throughout the rest of the day. Yet in some sense, we're always going into the unknown. To be sensible, we have to plan, but rather than trying to dominate life through an effort to seize control of it, we can plan knowing that things might well change and change again. If we enter the unknown with an open mind, we won't be mired in rage when our efforts at control are thwarted, and there will be room for love and compassion.

- **When our efforts to help seem futile, we can trust that in another time and place there may be unexpected results.** When we're trying to address a problem, improve the state of the world, help an alcoholic friend, comfort a grieving child, it might all appear to be going nowhere. Yet our actions are like planting seeds in the ground. We don't know for sure when they will bear fruit, and what looks like failure may be a time of gestation. Our work toward the good can be sustained if we don't harshly measure the success or failure of our actions by the immediate, and superficially apparent, results.

— **When we open to the present instead of resisting it, we find that we do have the strength to go on, step by step.** Even in times of immense suffering, we have the capacity to relate to the present moment in a way that keeps us from despairing. In fact, painful times can be an opportunity to find out what really is important to us. Pain wears away superficial concerns, leaving us with a powerful urge for freedom, happiness, and wholeness of being. When we are responsive to that urge, in every moment we can make a new beginning. Kindness toward ourselves in these times and circumstances becomes the springboard of kindness toward all of life.

Closing

We have an incredible capacity to wake up, to move through hesitations and patterns of withdrawal, to reach out to others and allow them to reach out to us. We have the ability to remember kindness as the genuine force of happiness that it is, no matter what circumstance we find ourselves in. We have the ability to face the ups and downs of every day, to come to terms with the transience of life, and to reach for the grace and uplifting nature of kindness. May we celebrate this capacity each day of our lives by working to make this capacity a reality. Kindness can heal our lives — and transform this world.

When we let things be as they are
The river of kindness rises to the
       surface of our lives.
One sip and the spirit is renewed …
Drink again.
Drink deeply.
That water will flow in your veins.
And you will become fearless …
Free to care about others
The way you care about your
       hands and feet.

KRISHNA DAS

Bibliography

Bhikkhu, Thanissaro. *The Buddha, on Skillfulness.* Translated from the Pali by Thanissaro Bhikkhu. Access to Insight edition © 2002 http://accesstoinsight.org.

Collins, Billy. *The Apple That Astonished Paris.* Fayetteville, AR: The University of Arkansas Press, 1996.

Dalai Lama, His Holiness. *Ethics for the New Millennium.* New York, NY: Penguin Putnam, The Berkley Publishing Group, Riverhead Books, 1999.

Dass, Ram. *Miracle of Love: Stories About Neem Karoli Baba,* compiled by Ram Dass. Santa Fe, NM: Hanuman Foundation, 1979, 1995.

King, Martin Luther Jr. "A Christmas Sermon on Peace." December 24, 1967. http://portland.indymedia.org.

King, Martin Luther Jr. "Loving Your Enemies." *A Knock at Midnight: Inspiration from the Great Sermons of Reverend Martin Luther King, Jr.* New York: Warner Books, 1998. http://www.stanford.edu.

Kyi, Aung San Suu, and Alan Clements. *The Voice of Hope,* updated and revised edition. New York: Seven Stories Press, 2008.

Kyi, Aung San Suu. *Freedom from Fear and Other Writings: Revised Edition.* New York: The Penguin Group, Penguin Putnam Inc., 1991, 1995.

Nye, Naomi Shihab. *Words Under the Words: Selected Poems.* Portland, OR: The Eighth Mountain Press, 1995.

Post, Stephen, and Jill Neimark. *Why Good Things Happen to Good People.* New York: Random House, Doubleday Broadway Publishing Group, Broadway Books, 2007.

Credits

The Metta Sutta is a translation of the Metta Sutta from Amaravati Publications.

The Three Elements of Self-Compassion and Self-Compassion Quiz from Dr. Kristin Neff's website: www.self-compassion.org — permission granted by Dr. Kristin Neff, Associate Professor in Human Development at the University of Texas at Austin.

Billy Collins, "Another Reason Why I Don't Keep A Gun In The House" from *The Apple That Astonished Paris.* Copyright ©1988, 1996 by Billy Collins. Used by permission of the University of Arkansas Press, www.uapress.com.

From "The Buddha, on anger" translated from the Pali by Thanissaro Bhikkhu. Verbal permission granted by Thanissaro Bhikkhu. From accesstoinsight.org. Copyright © 2002 Thanissaro Bhikkhu. Access to Insight edition © 2002.

"So Much Happiness" from *Words Under the Words: Selected Poems* by Naomi Shihab Nye, copyright © 1995. Reprinted with the permission of Far Corner Books, Portland, Oregon.

Special thanks to Krishna Das for the closing poem.

About the Author

SHARON SALZBERG has been leading meditation retreats worldwide since 1974. Influenced by her 35 years of study with Buddhist masters from a variety of traditions, she teaches intensive awareness practice ("insight" meditation) and the profound cultivation of lovingkindness and compassion. She is cofounder of the Insight Meditation Society and the Barre Center for Buddhist Studies, both in Massachusetts. Sharon Salzberg is the author of several books, including *The Force of Kindness; Faith; Lovingkindness;* and *A Heart as Wide as the World;* and the audio programs *Insight Meditation* (with Joseph Goldstein) and *Lovingkindness Meditation.*

About Sounds True

SOUNDS TRUE was founded in 1985 with a clear vision: to disseminate spiritual wisdom. Located in Boulder, Colorado, Sounds True publishes teaching programs that are designed to educate, uplift, and inspire. We work with many of the leading spiritual teachers, thinkers, healers, and visionary artists of our time.

To receive a free catalog of tools and teachings for personal and spiritual transformation, please visit www.soundstrue.com, call toll-free 800-333-9185, or write to us at the address below.

The Sounds True Catalog
PO Box 8010
Boulder, CO 80306